Bypass

John Queor

Indie Earth Publishing Inc.
| Miami, FL |

INDIE EARTH
PUBLISHING

Bypass

John Queor

Table of Contents

"My Darling
        Katherine Leneore"

My, Beautiful young darling,
   You give me goosepimples
And I think you have a heart of sterling.

When our special day comes.
   I hope your greatest dream
Will Come true with happiness
Which meets your highest esteem.

For I love you my beautiful one.
   My most meaning dream "plup",
I stomake you happy "HUN".
   And our time together will neverbe up.

And last of all honey
   OUR hearts willbe happy forever.
Because with a girl likeyou
   I will always bejoyous

                    By
                    Roger D.

I dedicate this book to my parents, the ones responsible for giving me my heart in the first place. I love you.

<table>
<tr><td>Patient Name:
  JOHN QUEOR</td><td></td><td>Procedure: BYPASS</td></tr>
<tr><td>Page: IX</td><td></td><td></td></tr>
</table>

CONSULTATION

"Coronary Artery Bypass Surgery creates a new path for blood to flow around a blocked or partially blocked artery in the heart. The surgery involves taking a healthy blood vessel from the chest or leg area. The vessel is connected below the blocked heart artery. The new pathway improves blood flow to the heart muscle."

Welcome to my procedure.

The following pages are memories, dreams, journal entries, battles, hopes, deep thoughts, wars, but most of all, love.

I am creating new channels so that love can flow into and through me again. I hope this medical journal is inspirational, interesting, and in some way, relatable to everyone reading.

*Warning: Do not read *Bypass* if you are pregnant or nursing, if your own sadness is overwhelming, if you are allergic to beautiful things, if you are sensitive to the sodium of your tears, if you are just incredibly sensitive, if cute things nauseate you, if you are in a successful marriage, if poetry throws you into fits of rage, or if you  hate Lana Del Rey.

<table>
<tr><td>Patient Name:
  JOHN QUEOR</td><td></td><td>Procedure: BYPASS</td></tr>
<tr><td>Page: 1</td><td></td><td>I AM A POET OF LOSS</td></tr>
</table>

I used to be a poet of love
Until I realized I'm not a lover
I'm a loner whose batteries had died
And selfishly I let someone hold me
Until I had fully become recharged
And now I'm just romanticizing
Men who have deep earthy eyes
And a cornucopia of issues
For me to realize and dive inside
So that I may heal them
And they can leave me
And I can be sad for a while
And scribble poetry of loss
So come on and lose me

Sometimes forever isn't
Siempre
Just a handful of moments
Carried around your neck
In the crevices and cracks
Of a clear quartz necklace

I watched it sprout
Moments after I met you
It bloomed beautifully
And then I felt it die

Sometimes forever isn't
Siempre
But we are caught in time
Cinematic moments
That can't be taken away
Even in fire or rain

Siempre: Spanish for 'always'

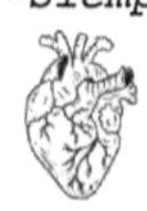

I don't want anyone to want me right now
Despite the reassurance I don't feel worthy
I am a bomb that can't stop exploding
No one has what it takes to clean this mess
There's a safety hidden within my loneliness
You cannot leave me if you are not here
I can sprawl all over my fresh black sheets
Without worrying about touching your skin
Wondering if my contact is lingering
If my toxins are causing you to itch
I don't want anyone to want me right now
I don't even want to be here but I have to be
The course is mandatory but I'm tired
I used to love love until I choked on it
It feels like a disorder to me now
As I practice in the bathroom mirror
Murmuring self-love affirmations
After I'm squeaky clean from a shower
And even at my cleanest
I still feel wrong to want it

One night I'll find myself awake
At 5:43 in the morning
But instead of wrestling the bed
I'll be locked in arms that love me
I'll find myself immensely relieved
When my eyes catch yours open

A sigh will sneak out like a cry
But it'll be a very happy expression
For it was a dream I had for years
That started out as a hopeful aspiration

Your crisp voice will coo to me
With some kind of playful profanity
As to why I always speak in my sleep
And why I mumble of hide and seek
And I'll slither deeper in your grasp
And explain that I found you at last

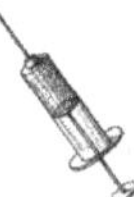

<table>
<tr><td>Patient Name:
JOHN QUEOR</td><td></td><td>Procedure: BYPASS</td></tr>
<tr><td>Page: 6</td><td></td><td>LOVE SONGS</td></tr>
</table>

My head is full of love songs
I'm sure it's just a love bomb
But I always ride the wave
Giddy with thoughts that swirl
Like thick plumes exhaled

My favorite part is when it's fresh
The anxiety and anticipation of
Arranging the building blocks
Into a tower meant to withstand
The earth when it begins to quake

I hum along to all the love songs
As I scribble in my journal furiously
Describing your eyes in great depth
Stuck in a web of wistful wonder
Of when the music will stop

I stay up all night
Trying to create plans
To preserve what I have
To seal my comfort away
In a glass box
Like a piece of royal jewelry
That I can gaze upon
And place upon myself
On holidays and
Special occasions
It's not realistic
Slowly I will lose everything
Deep down I know this
Selfishly I hope I'm first
I'm aware it could be worse
I know the storms are brewing
Bringing deafening thunder
And waves like citadel walls
That will humble me
For each time I truly believed
I was doing well
Or having any fun

<table>
<tr><td>Patient Name:
JOHN QUEOR</td><td></td><td>Procedure: BYPASS</td></tr>
<tr><td>Page: 8</td><td></td><td>I DO</td></tr>
</table>

I find myself saying
I used to
More than I say
I do

I don't think
I'll ever say
I do

But if ever
I do
It'll be something
I used to
Dream of

<table>
<tr><td>Patient Name:
  JOHN QUEOR</td><td></td><td>Procedure: BYPASS</td></tr>
<tr><td>Page: 10</td><td></td><td>**DARKROOM**</td></tr>
</table>

I'd spent years
Thinking of the ways
I could change
So you would see me
In the light I saw you
I melted in your warmth
Like wax in summer sun
I hardened
When you were gone
I broke all of the bulbs
I wouldn't have to change
If there was no light
To compare myself in

<table>
<tr><td>Patient Name:
JOHN QUEOR</td><td></td><td>Procedure: BYPASS</td></tr>
<tr><td>Page: 11</td><td></td><td>**TAKE ME OUT TONIGHT**</td></tr>
</table>

Take me out tonight

The bass is bouncing

Upon my windows

I feel like a caged bird

Be the wind beneath my wings

Could we chase midnight

Could you kiss me

Right before the sun rises

And then go away

Until I crave to leave

The cage again

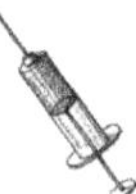

<table>
<tr><td>Patient Name:
JOHN QUEOR</td><td></td><td>Procedure: BYPASS</td></tr>
<tr><td>Page: 13</td><td></td><td>BLUE BEDROOM</td></tr>
</table>

I want your arms
To feel like my bedroom
With the blue walls
Doodled upon closet doors
And the zebra comforter
I've got fifteen years
Of pent up tears
And I want to cry at home

The world is broken
It is devastating
But it is not over
It will heal in time
And be hurt again
In an endless cycle
Like how the clouds
Sob until they vanish
To return again full
With brand new sorrows
To sprinkle on the land
The world is broken
It is devastating
It is necessary
To learn and grow
To collect our sorrows
To soak the earth in them
So hope has a place to grow
Like food that feeds the soul
And brings us back together
To gather around the table
To break bread and be thankful
That most things are fixable

| Patient Name:
JOHN QUEOR | | Procedure: BYPASS |
| Page: 15 | | **RISPERIDONE** |

It's almost always been
One-sided
I can be such a klutz
When I'm gazed upon
For but just a moment
But suddenly
They're on one knee
Presenting a ring
And we're married
Near a gorgeous river
And we're laughing
Splashing in the sea
And we're crossing
The threshold
Of a lovely colonial
And just as fast
They're tired of me
And we try
Therapy
And we fail
And they move out
And I sign the papers
And I sigh in relief...

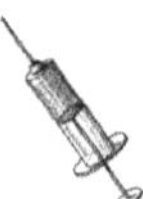

<table>
<tr><td>Patient Name:
JOHN QUEOR</td><td></td><td>Procedure: BYPASS</td></tr>
<tr><td>Page: 16</td><td></td><td>RISPERIDONE (CONT.)</td></tr>
</table>

. . .

Because all they've done

Is look at me

And I've dodged a bullet

Limbs intertwining isn't enough
For this kind of twisting vine
Where substance is the water
To this fertilized soil

Forming cracks from the lick
Of dry desert sunlight
Where once a great lake roamed
But was used up in his youth

Orange warmth felt nice
Until it turned everything brown
The lush vine died without the lake
And the sun had no one to entertain

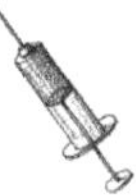

It's terribly difficult
To not feel terrible
About all the time
That's swirled the drain
I could have been
Much more vocal
About my emptiness
But I'm sure you knew
I can only imagine
You seeing it clearly
As I looked back at you
But I still feel terrible
It lingers inside of me
A burrowing parasite
On borrowed time
I hope you're fine
I hope all good things
Fall upon your lap
And going forth
You never feel
Terrible

<table>
<tr><td>Patient Name:
JOHN QUEOR</td><td></td><td>Procedure: BYPASS</td></tr>
<tr><td>Page: 19</td><td></td><td>LOST</td></tr>
</table>

To be honest
I've discovered
I don't wish
To be found

I'm scattered
In the skyline
Steeping
In the sea
Sleeping
In the clouds
On the branches
Of trees

I'll find a nomad
With a heart
With wings
Who will be
Just as lost
As me

Fleeting are my white lace dreams
of aisles of blood-red roses guiding
Two lives into one grand eternity
Glimmering like a polished diamond
Clasped hand in hand not clammy
But passionate and exuberant

Candles floating in frosted vases
Two figurines sitting atop a cake
Vows to keep each other afloat
Vows to keep each other great

Scrapbook plans for a beautiful evening
Surrounded by love and twinkle lights
Aspirations of his and his first dance
But since you nothing's ever felt right
My white lace dreams are fading
They get blurrier every night

<table>
<tr><td>Patient Name:
  JOHN QUEOR</td><td></td><td>Procedure: BYPASS</td></tr>
<tr><td>Page: 22</td><td></td><td>PARASITIC</td></tr>
</table>

I like it when you say my name
When you catch my gaze
And then you take it away
The insidious smile on your face
The innocence caught in amber orbs
That we both know is fake

I like it when you say my name
The way you wet your bottom lip
The leftover dew from your drink
Your tongue flickers like a snake
And I feel like I could be prey
And I don't mind a wink

I like it when you say my name
I want to hear it in a softer tone
Cocooned in the blackness of my sheets
Where you could finally sink your teeth
Into my moon-kissed vanilla glow
And feed until you explode

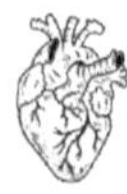

<table>
<tr><td>Patient Name:
JOHN QUEOR</td><td></td><td>Procedure: BYPASS</td></tr>
<tr><td>Page: 23</td><td></td><td>SAVE A HORSE,
RIDE A COWBOY</td></tr>
</table>

I always felt like I was
Part of a teen drama
Lying in bed crying over boys
I had a massive
Edward Cullen poster
Next to my bed with
The zebra comforter
And a picture on the
Opposing wall that said
"Save a horse,
Ride a cowboy"
My dad hated that one

I filled barrels
With those sadnesses
They commanded my pen
I was convinced one of them
Would be a happy ending

I always felt like I was
Such a loser for...

<table>
<tr><td>Patient Name:
JOHN QUEOR</td><td></td><td>Procedure: BYPASS</td></tr>
<tr><td>Page: 24</td><td></td><td>**SAVE A HORSE,
RIDE A COWBOY** (CONT.)</td></tr>
</table>

. . .

Lying in bed crying over boys

Letting my heart beat too fast

Romanticizing crumbs

Into bountiful loaves of bread

"Save a horse

Ride a cowboy"

My dad hated that one

Two hearts in the dark
Searching for the light
On opposite sides
Your below is above me
I don't feel the warmth yet
Do you feel me reaching
Whose gravity is heavier
I've been falling forever

<table>
<tr><td>Patient Name:
  JOHN QUEOR</td><td></td><td>Procedure: BYPASS</td></tr>
<tr><td>Page: 27</td><td></td><td>**AMNESIA**</td></tr>
</table>

I forget

That

You must also

Give love to yourself

Or

You'll fall asleep

And wake up

Twenty years later

Not knowing

Who you are

Where you are

What you want

Or how you got here

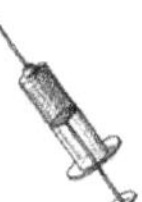

When I was a younger soul
I always did as I was told
I feared defiance
And the scold that would follow
On my knees before my bed
I closed my eyes and words bled
From my lips requesting forgiveness
As years passed on and souls ascended
Into the abyss they swore lied
Beyond the stars that
Looked like shards to
A puzzle destroyed
I pondered and wondered
And questioned my faith

Wrinkled faces and souls
Much older than my own
Told me that my destiny I did not own
But the father who lived in the abyss
Above the stars that looked like shards
Created a plan before I was born
A path was drawn before my first dawn
And I had to follow...

<table>
<tr><td>Patient Name:
JOHN QUEOR</td><td></td><td>Procedure: BYPASS</td></tr>
<tr><td>Page: 29</td><td></td><td>THE PHASE CONTINUES (CONT.)</td></tr>
</table>

. . .

On my knees before my bed
I could not find the words to speak
Inside I had been tainted
By hatred that haunted me
I no longer felt a divine connection
Just rejection

I knew from a young age
That I was very strange
They told me it was just a phase
But I knew better
Father would be disappointed
If he knew the things I wanted to do
I feared myself and my damnation
If I decided to follow through
And do as my heart told me to
A handsome demon with angelic eyes
Stared with me into the sky
We searched the constellations
While shooting stars passed by

The sky was midnight violet
The first time I kissed him
I remember believing that
All of the wars were worth it
Just to have his brown eyes
Pause and look deeply into mine
I figured we'd go to college together
Live artistically and scandalously
Lost in a united cloud of dreaming
To wake up to him kissing me
In the lavender hue of early morning
I put him so far ahead of myself
Never anticipating the departure
And everything I found in him
He took with him into the wind
My sand castles were destroyed
My time capsules were worthless now
And every time the sky was violet
I hated myself for losing myself
In pyrite eyes that didn't choose me
But stayed elevated in the substances
As I swirled the drain

I knocked over the first domino
When I was beneath you
In the unmade twin bed
With your tears crashing onto me
You had two cool blue pools
It was a scorching summer then
But I should have ran away
I was baptized and damned
Almost simultaneously
As your frame piled upon me
Your lips crawled upon me
Your fingers dragged upon me
And I stayed beneath you
Sometimes I'm still beneath you
Your hands as vines
Wrapped around my wrists
You had a poisonous kiss

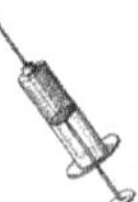

Angel
Might I return
Your wings to you
Some place quiet
Just us two
You've been living
The same as I have
I saw it in your eyes
I believe they branded me
I'll wear it with wonder
When will you return
To exist in my seasons
Not as a scene
Haphazard
Disheveled

<table>
<tr><td>Patient Name:
  JOHN QUEOR</td><td></td><td>Procedure: BYPASS</td></tr>
<tr><td>Page: 33</td><td></td><td>**TICKET**</td></tr>
</table>

I slept with
A Dunkin Donuts
Supervisor
When I moved home
From the darkest point
Of my life
And I thought
He might be my light
My one way ticket
Out of the ice
I plunged back into
I saw my breath
Each morning
Like I was the child
From The Sixth Sense
But I wasn't being
Haunted by the dead
I was trapped
In the purgatory
Inside my head
And he wasn't
The ticket
Out

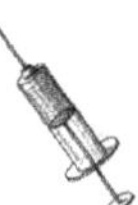

<table>
<tr><td>Patient Name:
  JOHN QUEOR</td><td></td><td>Procedure: BYPASS</td></tr>
<tr><td>Page: 34</td><td></td><td>**SNOW IN SPRING**</td></tr>
</table>

I remember the snow in spring
You smiled like a child
Ecstatic on Christmas morning
A lone flake dissolving
On the tip of your tongue
I thought I had it all
My solitude was dissolving
Like an ice sculpture
Trapped in humidity
I still feel the naivety
The chill in my bones
When you taught me
The true nature of cruelty
And why I can never let go
Even when swaddled
In fine silk comfort
Even when wrapped
In familiar arms
Even when wrapped
In my own

Perhaps I wasn't
cut in two
when in a bout of rage
did Zeus
Split all of us
from ourselves
I fear I've searched
all these years
for something
I already had
inside
sunshine

My heart lives a decade behind me
In a town I could not wait to escape
In a house I was forced to flee from
But at the time didn't mind running from
To come back to what was my home
But was actually a frozen wasteland
That I tossed in a blender with mint
And enough rum to be numb for ten years
My heart lives in a slew of chests
Of men that I would have given anything
To be loved the way that I had loved them
They are scattered now in many winds
That my whispers have gotten lost in
My sky sometimes feels so starless
But slowly I'm finding pieces of light
To decorate the darkness surrounding
My heart is being called to return to me
The fragments and slivers will come home
To a comfort they've barely known
One day we will be whole again

<table>
<tr><td>Patient Name:
  JOHN QUEOR</td><td></td><td>Procedure: BYPASS</td></tr>
<tr><td>Page: 38</td><td></td><td>MY SKIN WILL
BETRAY ME</td></tr>
</table>

My skin will betray me
Joining forces with gravity
To drag me towards the earth
Exhausting my elasticity
Like an abused rubber band

My collection of years
Will stand on my shoulders
Forcing me to slouch
Hopefully not as severely
As my great grandma Blair

My bones will betray me too
Brittle like sweet peanut candy
Crumbling beneath the weight
Of all the stars above me
And the atmosphere

Waiting for me to leave

MR. AND MRS. LEROY BLAIR

<table>
<tr><td>Patient Name:
JOHN QUEOR</td><td></td><td>Procedure: BYPASS</td></tr>
<tr><td>Page: 41</td><td></td><td>GHOST STORY</td></tr>
</table>

How will I know when
I've finally found you
I've been wrong before
I peered into their eyes
Searching for intention
I've walked inside their minds

Am I meant to meander
Alone like a ghost forever
If I truly believed that
I'd probably feel better
Less foolish than hoping
I could be held forever

I don't recall much softness
Beyond the sheets
Before I chose to freeze
And that ruins me
And that creates me
The creature
Who romanticizes
Everything

I've been in love
Five times this week
And I don't even
Know their names

As I peel off the wallpaper
I immediately wish to replaster
Not one facet of my entire life
Is as magical as I try to believe
And that ruins me
And that creates me
The creature
Who romanticizes
Everything

I fell in love with a boy
Who wouldn't kiss me
He utilized my lips
Just as I found use for his
But he wouldn't kiss me

I held him
But he didn't feel it
I loved him
But he didn't want it

I fell in love with a boy
Who vanished into the horizon
He utilized my lips
But he never read them
As I whispered

Don't leave

I shattered my own heart
I collected all of the shards
I created a mosaic
Like glass graffiti
Smooth to the eyes
But extremely sharp
Like barbed wire
Sometimes
It feels like a prison
Confining me
But also a blessing
By keeping you out
My dreams are too drastic
They take me so far away
I'm always in shock
When I'm finally able to wake
To gaze through the glass graffiti
And lightly touch the thorns
Keeping you away
Keeping me within

I saw a scorpion when I closed my eyes
And then reminisced on your sting
And how the venom wouldn't set in
I licked the wound and carried on
Because there was no other choice

Blue flashes of hypnotic eyes
Chemicals glimmering on your lips
And I suckled at your wound
Supple skin tasting like poison
And I refused to spit

Unwavering obsessions settled
I shook myself from that state
Cravings to be endlessly wanted
Subsided and the substances did too
I run neither to or from you

Might you be a serpent
To wrap me so tightly
In your arms, torso, and legs
Not so tightly to
Crush my bones
Not so lightly that I
Wriggle free and flee
Semi-uncomfortably
So I tire myself quickly
So that I stop fighting
Letting my tears of rage
Plummet into our earth
Creating mighty craters
Like the scars on my skin
I'll let you read like braille
And when my sobs subside
I will let you in
If you'd still like
To be invited

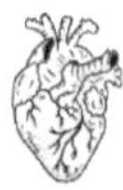

I scoured my bedroom
Praying you left a shirt behind
I wasn't ready to let go
When you ascended upward
To spend a little time in the clouds
That my mind spent most of its time in

I cried and wished
You would have held me
Like the jaws of life
And not boarded because
I knew you weren't coming back

I'm embarrassed to admit
How many stupid pockets
I slipped my heart into
Like a phone number
Scribbled on a napkin
Forgotten about and
Put on the spin cycle

<table>
<tr><td>Patient Name:
  JOHN QUEOR</td><td></td><td>Procedure: BYPASS</td></tr>
<tr><td>Page: 50</td><td></td><td>BLACK ICE</td></tr>
</table>

April flakes

Divine dandruff

Our breaths

Swirled into one

You were colder

Unnoticeable

Black ice

Too smooth

Too invasive

Corrosive

Venomous

I saw you

In my own light

You were cardboard

Illuminated

Like the Hollywood sign

By my projection

<table>
<tr><td>Patient Name:
JOHN QUEOR</td><td></td><td>Procedure: BYPASS</td></tr>
<tr><td>Page: 51</td><td></td><td>FAILING AT LOVE</td></tr>
</table>

I've gotten

Further

Ahead

By

Failing

At love

Because

Being alone

Gave me

The shove

I needed

To love

Who I've been

This whole time

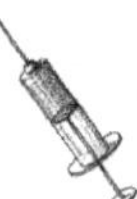

Maybe everything isn't as cool
As I ushered you to believe
But it's not your business anymore
I'm a lone star in the vastness
Screaming out with no audience
I think I prefer it this way

My pain cannot be weaponized
Instead it's stagnant in the wine cellar
Where there is no longer any wine
It was depleted in a feeding frenzy
The last time I cried until sunrise
Held somewhat comfortably

I heard that healing isn't linear
It slopes and curves like cursive
Like letters written and then burned
A message in the chemtrails
The way tears escape the chin
The way it used to be your business

<table>
<tr><td>Patient Name:
  JOHN QUEOR</td><td></td><td>Procedure: BYPASS</td></tr>
<tr><td>Page: 53</td><td></td><td>MARLBORO RED
HUNDREDS</td></tr>
</table>

Tears tasted like

Pabst blue ribbon

Sat out overnight

Sixteen ounce pounder

Cigarette butt roughly

Stuffed through that

Small can opening

To sip from

In the morning

Another long night

Spent mostly crying

Waking up thirsty

Long drawn drink

Pulling black bits

Of wet tobacco

From my teeth

Only those tears

Ever tasted like

Cigarette soaked

Beer

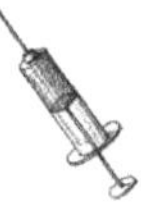

⟨TCWRE⟩

He taps on the screen door
not out of respect
But
to taunt me
to remind me
That
He is out there
With
Heart shaped pupils
wide and fixated
Waiting
to destroy my home
again

There's an ache inside
It's meek and agoraphobic
It's inside making a mess
My walls feel box-dye black
It's going to take a little bit
To get it sky blue again
I know it's right beyond the clouds
But my breath won't reach
When I exhale to sigh or scream
It only stretches a few feet
And I can't help but feel defeated
To feel that deep aching
The patch of very deep black
Covering one eye at all times

Am I cruel and unusual
For refusing his love
Thrown on me resembling
A very heavy quilt but
So cold as snow

Fingers against my flesh
I couldn't find my breath
Not in a fairytale romantic way
But like being held beneath water
Unable to see the surface

No one will ever love me
In such a way as he
But my lips were blue
And eyes were crashing
Alone in his stormy sea

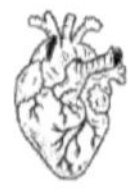

<table>
<tr><td>Patient Name:
JOHN QUEOR</td><td></td><td>Procedure: BYPASS</td></tr>
<tr><td>Page: 58</td><td></td><td>**GEORGIA O'KEEFFE**</td></tr>
</table>

I think I saw the woman
You will leave me for
I can see your reflection
Growing in her eyes
And I think she's a lion
And I know she is hungry

I think she will be your freedom
From having to slowly slosh around
These murky waters we let overflow
With your soft hand on my hard shoulder

I think I saw the woman
You will leave me for
I can feel you start to drift
And we are at a crossroads
Meeting in the middle
To burn all the roses

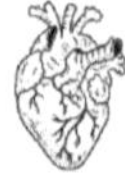

<table>
<tr><td>Patient Name:
JOHN QUEOR</td><td></td><td>Procedure: BYPASS</td></tr>
<tr><td>Page: 59</td><td></td><td>FLOP</td></tr>
</table>

My champagne is flat
This doesn't feel like a party anymore
More of a mourning but
We are still breathing
Floating on a mattress and
The air is escaping
My hands are going numb
I'm covered in hives
And the room is silent
Other than the fan
And it all feels so wrong
Especially remembering when
It all felt so beautiful
My heart feels like cement
And I've fallen in an ocean
I'm enveloped in deep cool
I need to blow out the candles
Save the mess for the morning
Untether the balloons
And let Judy Garland twirl
Atop the turntable
To consume my blue

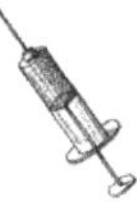

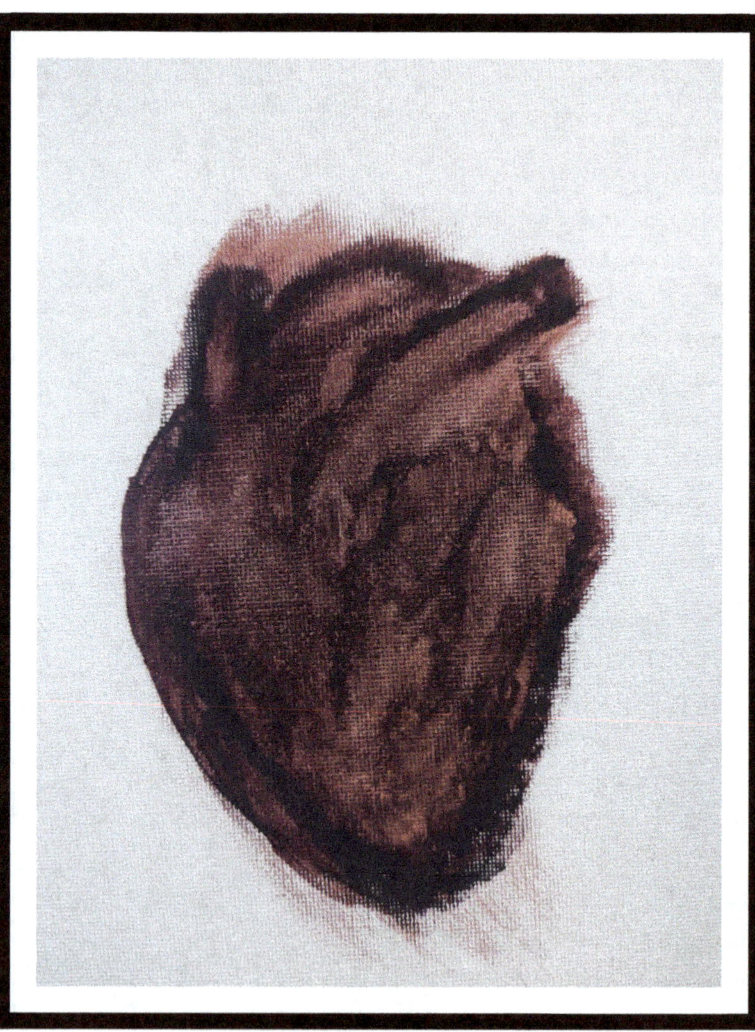

<table>
<tr><td>Patient Name:
  JOHN QUEOR</td><td></td><td>Procedure: BYPASS</td></tr>
<tr><td>Page: 61</td><td></td><td>**CORONARY ARTERY**</td></tr>
</table>

I thought my poetry
Was enough processing
And things would return
To flowing normally
I thought that somehow
With my introspective soothing
I could wake up each day
Unscathed
But that's not the case
There are flutters
Small palpitations
Shortness of breath
Pixelated dreams
Of all of the things
That I truly wanted
And all of the things
That went away

<table>
<tr><td>Patient Name:
  JOHN QUEOR</td><td></td><td>Procedure: BYPASS</td></tr>
<tr><td>Page: 62</td><td></td><td>**STRIKE**</td></tr>
</table>

Saline sliding down

Two lonesome trails

From cheek to chin

Heart to heart

Your words warm

My stare cold

Running in circles

Because we know

The end is near

Getting close

To curtains close

Rose petals dispersed

And doused

In gasoline

Clutching tightly to

Our matchbooks

Fighting in slow motion

Trying to decide

Who will be the villain

And strike

I'll look at you
And even if I'm not too keen
I'll wish you well
I'll whisper inside of myself
An uplifting prayer
Blurbs to leave the atmosphere
Multiply in size
Mirror all the star shards
Consume crumbs of their light
And once more plummet down
Friction melting them into liquid
Winter turning them into stone
To slip smoothly into your pocket
To later melt into your skin
To be gifted to an unsuspecting
Soul who needs a flash of light
Like those ribbons in the north

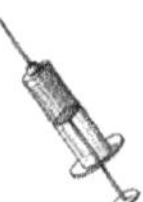

<table>
<tr><td>Patient Name:
JOHN QUEOR</td><td></td><td>Procedure: BYPASS</td></tr>
<tr><td>Page: 64</td><td></td><td>SCIENCE</td></tr>
</table>

I'm keeping the last drop in the drawer
Beside me inside my bedside table
Where once both of our things littered
Atop that cheap Ikea wrongly assembled
Square that posed as a treasure chest
And doubled as dining table and trash can

The last drop of romantic feelings
That weren't dead on impact upon
The drunken uselessly endless aggressive
Words spat sitting at the kitchen table
Where I was fighting to be numb
And you were fighting to be loved

When I'm healthy enough to gear out of
Autopilot and back into attempting to try
Accepting the rush of human experience
I can put that drop under a microscope
And get a bit experimental with how to love
Without purposely trying to drown myself

I don't want to be your last love
I'm just a filler in your timeline
A collection of memories to visit
Smile and then snuggle deeper
Into the arms of the one for you

I'm not the one to meet you at the altar
Flowers cascading and bubbles rising
Buttercream three-tiered fruit-filled
Smeared on a gleaming grin ear to ear
Dancing to soft music as the sun sets

I don't want to be your last love
My butterflies have all passed away
I'm just lingering waiting for the chop
For you to realize that I just am not
The one you will end your story with

Blockages forming
Yearning for a
Partial opening
Arrhythmic beating
Stealing the stars from
Someone else's sky

<table>
<tr><td>Patient Name:
  JOHN QUEOR</td><td></td><td>Procedure: BYPASS</td></tr>
<tr><td>Page: 70</td><td></td><td>POTPOURRI</td></tr>
</table>

I think of love
I think of it often
How close I got
How far I am now
I am desolate
The lights flicker
Like the open sign
In a gas station window
In the middle of nowhere
Dilapidated
Overlooked
With dead flies
Sprinkled like potpourri
Covered in ash
And malt liquor
I think it'll stop soon
Strobing for attention
I think I get it
I'll give it up
Batting my lashes
Dreaming
Wishing on you

Two feels more lonely than one
The party hats smell of mildew and
I can't get comfortable in this bed
Where you sit stagnant staring at me
Waiting for the right time to strike
But there never is a right time

It's passed the point of awkward now
My skin wants to escape my bones
Aspirations to liquefy and seep through
The sheets and into any nearby drain
It's unseen pain burning white and blue
Nothing really tarnished or bruised

I wish I knew where it all went
The feelings that once danced inside me
When I was content watching the sun rise
With you watching it rise with me
Now the curtains are always closed
And I'd evaporate given the opportunity

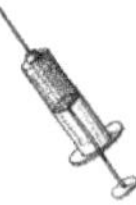

What haunts me in the daylight
Caressing breezes like breaths
Wrapping lightly around my neck
But tightening in small increments
As I fall backwards in mounds of snow
I knew you could be so cold
I used to look into your eyes
I followed you through seasons
Backseat car rides singing
Skin blistering in the summer sun
I would chase and you would run
Endless discussions beneath the moon
I think my dreams are coming true
You've fallen so far behind me now
But I still think of you
Of our smoke rings conjoining
Of my dreams all those years ago
Before I knew how good it could get
Surfing through a sea of couches
And losing you to their depths

These dreams do not satiate
They slither in the darkness
To recenter and salivate
Cravings do not dissipate
But simmer after rising
Invasive imagery
Grinding hard into
Against the frontal lobe
With pleading eyes
Eager tongue flicking
Your scent lingers
Even after waking
Reaching out for
My dark phantom
Taking me to Sodom
And then leaving me
In Gomorrah

<table>
<tr><td>Patient Name:
JOHN QUEOR</td><td></td><td>Procedure: BYPASS</td></tr>
<tr><td>Page: 75</td><td></td><td>GLANCE</td></tr>
</table>

I'm fine to sit and watch as you
Brightly light up an entire room
Pacifying my endless thoughts
Of our impending doom
And it's fine if I may never
Taste the nectar of your fruits
Or build a lovely monument
Where you've put down your roots
It's okay if our fingers are
Never encircled in golden rings
I wish to never be attached
To any sort of tangible things
As I lie and think of you
I truly do not wish to possess
I'd much rather hold tight
To mutually adore and caress
I may never have you
In any sort of endless ways
But the sun never stops shining
Despite the clouds taking his rays
And I can fall in love with you
Each time I see your smile
No matter how sporadic
If only a short while

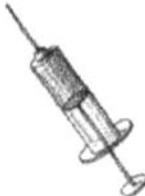

I hope there's one more for me
Last night I lingered in old echoes
My skin wanted someone to rest on
My eyes burned and I wanted to sleep
I stayed up until six writing poetry
I hope there's one more for me
Maybe not exactly right now
I've got more walls to take down
But at some point around the bend
Send someone that I can spend
The rest of what time I have here
I hope there's one more for me

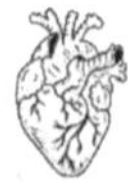

I'll set up a kissing booth
In a field of wildflowers
Way out of the way
Hours from the city's twinkle

There'll be grass in the lemonade
And I'll twist fresh flowers in my hair

I'll set up a kissing booth
In a field of fragrant flowers
Way out of the way
Where I've never been before

Just a quarter for one kiss
Just a minute or longer

I'll ask each one if by chance
They happen to be a Cancer
Terrence says I'll end up with one
I guess we'll see in the summer

I spent an hour
Searching for the calm
That slipped away
In the nighttime

I always find it

Usually at sunrise
The pale blue
Plowing the way
For melted gold

I always find it

If it stayed with me
I wouldn't appreciate it
So I watch it slip away
And then I start to panic

But I always find it

I watch each door open
With subtle anticipation
That my doves have guided
You back home

I watch each door close
With a feeling of emptiness
Just beyond desolate
A dull ache way down below

I watch the sun climb
I watch it slide to the other side
Horrified as the sting grows
Maybe you aren't coming home

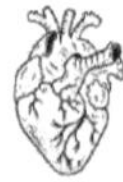

<table>
<tr><td>Patient Name:
JOHN QUEOR</td><td></td><td>Procedure: BYPASS</td></tr>
<tr><td>Page: 83</td><td></td><td>VACANT</td></tr>
</table>

Too long since skin cells
Descended onto my own
Where hot heavy air
Swirled in a vortex of two
Shallow breathing and
Patience fanned the flame

Soft lips exhale hard words
The heart is black and blue

Too long since nails dragged
Against this pale lit temple
But time has been spent inside
The candles jump with rage
Burning this chest hollow
The vacancy sign glows red

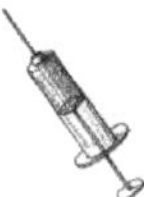

<table>
<tr><td>Patient Name:
  JOHN QUEOR</td><td></td><td>Procedure: BYPASS</td></tr>
<tr><td>Page: 84</td><td></td><td>**DESECRATED VINEYARDS**</td></tr>
</table>

In an alternative universe
Two glasses clink together
Sauvignon Blanc paired with
Delicious garden picked
Raw dogging in moonlight
Smile stretching from
Sea all the way to sky

Arms wrap my expanse
Twinkling in your glance
As our eyes sleepily together
Watch the sun claim the sky
With birds softly singing
A lullaby to drift away into
Champagne bubble dreaming

In an alternate universe
My dreams did bear fruit
Sweet from green lush vines
Aging with finesse like wine...

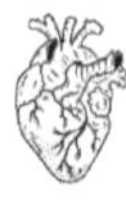

<table>
<tr><td>Patient Name:
JOHN QUEOR</td><td></td><td>Procedure: BYPASS</td></tr>
<tr><td>Page: 86</td><td></td><td>**DESECRATED VINEYARDS**
(CONT.)</td></tr>
</table>

...

Sometimes I go back to visit
Where sky collides with sea
To scribble letters into bottles

Letters you will never read

Where do I go from here
Diving in this ocean of change
Sending bubble messages to
Float and burst at the surface
Where your silhouette
No longer lingers leaving me
A bit uneasy with my own mind
Wondering if while submerged
You'd offer a hand to drag me from
The refreshing wet depths
Or hold me down to drown

I would have been fine with either
I would have been fine with either
I would have been fine with either

Now I'm fine with neither
I'll climb to the soil on my own
I'll sun bathe on the beach
Until I'm completely dry
I'll be absolutely fine
It's just a matter of time
Until I'm saturated in weakness...

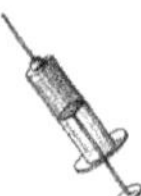

<table>
<tr><td>Patient Name:
JOHN QUEOR</td><td></td><td>Procedure: BYPASS</td></tr>
<tr><td>Page: 88</td><td></td><td>HONEYMOON(CONT.)</td></tr>
</table>

...

Etching a heart in new sand
Walking together hand in hand
Drowning after the honeymoon

It felt like a rash
The loneliness I let
Crash over me in waves
My skin got used
To brushing fingers
Embraces

My mind left first
Then my heart
And then my skin
There's no venom
Inside of me
I am whole
The slate is clean
Again

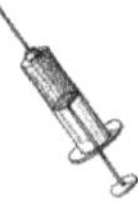

I wanted to
Run away
To the coast
His eyes on the road
My eyes on his lips
The curving of his smile
And his eyes
Catching mine
When he'd turn his head
Towards me

I built a castle of dreams
But I never saw myself inside
I was just the blueprint
Never the resident

I wanted to
Preserve myself
In that town
Accept the chokehold...

<table>
<tr><td>Patient Name:
 JOHN QUEOR</td><td></td><td>Procedure: BYPASS</td></tr>
<tr><td>Page: 91</td><td></td><td>**BLUEPRINT** (CONT.)</td></tr>
</table>

...

Of an incredibly simple life
Because he told me
I could trust him
I was on the balcony then
When
He smiled as he pushed me
Over the edge

A little stout man
Sat upon the pine
Requesting a burger
And an Arnold Palmer
He was simple
Much older than I
He had a certain kindness
That I forgot existed
Since my grandpa's departure
I've been numb to the absence
Never really thinking of it
Or reflecting on his ways
Until a little stout man
Sat upon the pine
And I couldn't help
But to see Bruce
As they smiled the same way

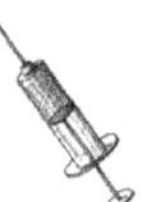

<table>
<tr><td>Patient Name:
  JOHN QUEOR</td><td></td><td>Procedure: BYPASS</td></tr>
<tr><td>Page: 94</td><td></td><td>THE SUMMIT</td></tr>
</table>

It's in a locked box now
Tucked under my bed
Like a forgotten earring
A gas station receipt
A single strand of hair
I don't intend to keep it there
Indefinitely
Only
Long enough to forget
What can happen
when you open up
And then swiftly shut
Like a gated community

8. 24. 23

I am somewhere hidden in
a bouquet of dead roses
lightly spritzed with
the pungency of Valerian root
and soft hopefulness of Jasmine
I am not the petals
Nor am I the stems or leaves
I am a blade
severing
I had dreams to be
arranged as a heart
on the mattress
but now I
sit in the foyer
and keep to myself

I have a drawer
of hidden dreams
that I know
are not meant for me
it hurts to watch them
fly away
but
in my heart
they can not stay
I am a free bird
I am a lone bird
I know it's all
the same

<table>
<tr><td>Patient Name:
  JOHN QUEOR</td><td></td><td>Procedure: BYPASS</td></tr>
<tr><td>Page: 97</td><td></td><td>BLUE</td></tr>
</table>

I've made investments

Folded pieces of me

To play as pocket squares

Like a quilt for the heart

I'm always misplaced

There's too much duality

I'm caught in the center

It seems everyone else

Either floats or sinks

But I stay still

I wrapped my heart

In fire-red twine

Until it began to burn

I've cooled down since then

My blood doesn't boil

The birds do not sing

There is no sunset

It's all ice blue

I started my Christmas shopping
A Johnny Cash clock for Dad
Perfume and a blanket for Mom
A tool kit for my little brother
Nice cologne for the other
And there's nothing for you
And I feel a little empty
I feel a jagged sting of sadness
That swiftly morphs into anger
Because it was always so fun
To watch your face light up
With joy and appreciation
But I won't see that this year
I won't see that next year
It's a very lonely journey to heal
To watch your name fall so quickly
To the very bottom of my messages
Where we had once exchanged
At least a million words
Back and forth...

...
To not at all
I hope you find the sunlight
I hope you are enveloped in peace
I hope you receive a fantastic slew
Of pretty wrapped gifts on Christmas
But above all else
I truly hope you're well

<table>
<tr><td>Patient Name:
  JOHN QUEOR</td><td></td><td>Procedure: BYPASS</td></tr>
<tr><td>Page: 100</td><td></td><td>**BITTEN**</td></tr>
</table>

I am not immune to my own venom
My veins burn on the New Moon
As I shed my skin and slither to the shower
I regurgitate my darkness into the drain
If there's one thing I know it's pain
The lava trickles down from my forehead
Cascading from my chest to my knees
I could recollect until the wells went dry
I could lie in the shower until I was dust
I am not immune to my own venom
The pendulum swings both ways
I am also chiseled at by the words I say
The feelings I let feast on my stomach
The memories developing in the dark room
That somehow I've lost access to
But something is stirring behind that door
With teeth just as hollow as my own
To puncture and release its load
To which there is no known antidote

The seven of Saturn
Worn like diadems
Not wedding rings
With seven different flowers
As the place holders
For the celebration table
To soon be covered
In lychee fruit and pomegranates
Spring water with cucumber
And seven deep red candles
Anointed with wild rose oil
It took many robberies
Before I found myself empty
But I am filled with star fire again
And after a treacherous storm
It takes a village

I cut a vein from my leg
And attached it to my heart
So that I could flow as I did
Before each of the blows
But I'm sitting at a crossroads
Evaluating what it is that I want
In comparison to what I actually need
I've found solace in being free
And hearing such a strong beat
Inspires me to stay far away
From fire and other dangerous things
But I know that too much safety
Is only living and not being alive
I know that poets chase love
Until we die

<table>
<tr><td>Patient Name:
JOHN QUEOR</td><td></td><td>Procedure: BYPASS</td></tr>
<tr><td>Page: 105</td><td></td><td>**I WILL NEVER HAVE
WHAT THEY HAVE**</td></tr>
</table>

I will never have what they have
I don't think it's in my design plan
A more solitary walk on the beach for me
Not even footsteps trailing behind me
The divine is letting me freefall
Swan diving into the cool darkness
Of a deprivation chamber
Forcing me to watch hallucinations
Where my very mundane desires
Appear before me as holographs
I've watched my whole life
A few inches behind myself
Like a cameraman

<table>
<tr><td>Patient Name:
  JOHN QUEOR</td><td></td><td>Procedure: BYPASS</td></tr>
<tr><td>Page: 106</td><td></td><td>BYPASS II.</td></tr>
</table>

How does your heart feel
Do you ever feel stuck in the middle
Do you still feel it breaking
Or are you healing
Or are you blessed enough
To be whole
With gleaming eyes that exude
A sense of wonder and confidence
When questioning 'what if'

I believed humans could
Only truly love four people
One per heart's quadrant
I think I may have cheated
I have loved more than four

My chest tightens when I think
Of the eyes I lost myself in
Creating space inside of myself
Knowing it wasn't reciprocated
But love doesn't care about fair...

<table>
<tr><td>Patient Name:
JOHN QUEOR</td><td></td><td>Procedure: BYPASS</td></tr>
<tr><td>Page: 108</td><td></td><td>BYPASS II. (CONT.)</td></tr>
</table>

...
It sits
It stays
It waits
For a
Bypass

<table>
<tr><td>Patient Name:
  JOHN QUEOR</td><td></td><td>Procedure: BYPASS</td></tr>
<tr><td>Page: 109</td><td></td><td>**SORCERY**</td></tr>
</table>

He's got the kind of eyes
You accidentally fall into
Like losing your footing
On a fragile ledge of gravel
You slide quickly down
Into two warm pools
That at first are angry
But smooth instantly
Like fresh maple syrup
Sticky and gripping
Flirtatiously manipulative
Naturally captivating
Like a siren's song
And before too long
You've drowned
And he blinks
And he's won

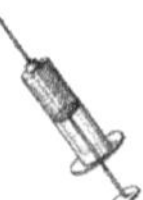

<table>
<tr><td>Patient Name:
  JOHN QUEOR</td><td></td><td>Procedure: BYPASS</td></tr>
<tr><td>Page: 111</td><td></td><td>SOULMATE</td></tr>
</table>

Could my soulmate be
A tree in a field all alone
Or a street painter in Paris
Or an opulent Arabian king

Could my soulmate be
A stone in a babbling brook
Or a wise old widower
Or a shaggy urban panhandler

Could my soulmate be
Also trying to search for me
Or has the world made them hard
Or has someone put out their flame

Could my soulmate be
The complete opposite of me
Or are we eerily similar
Or do we not even care

Could my soulmate be
Here sooner than later
Or do I have to wait forever
Or do they just not exist

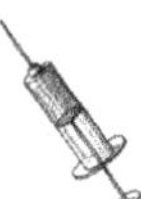

The sky is falling
Would you catch it
In your open palms
Like snow or ash

Would you exhale
A breath of life
Upon the ruins
Posing as piles of dust

Would you pull up a chair
Millimeters away from me
To watch it all end
The same as it began

The sky is falling
Put it in your pocket
A morsel to savor for later
When we're home again

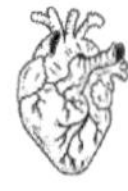

I wish to be kissed
In the middle of *Venice Bitch*
Within her hypnotic tones
And soft strumming
A smile spreading on your face
Because I'm humming

When I'm not so hard
I dream to be held
Like a star in your palm
That you whisper
Your wishes to

I wish to be kissed
In the middle of *Venice Bitch*
Within the glory of the outro
And right after you'll go
So I can dream to be held
Despite having been

<table>
<tr><td>Patient Name:
JOHN QUEOR</td><td></td><td>Procedure: BYPASS</td></tr>
<tr><td>Page: 115</td><td></td><td>BANANA CHOCOLATE CHIP PANCAKES</td></tr>
</table>

Half of me wishes
That a head was rested
On my chest right now
Our breaths coming
And going so slowly
As we fall into dreaming

Half of me wishes
That I'd hear music
Coming from the kitchen
And he was cooking
A stack of banana
Chocolate chip pancakes

Half of me feels alone
But I know it's necessary
I have to learn
To love myself in the quiet
To love myself in the daylight
Before anyone ever stays the night

Again

I blew a ring of smoke
It morphed into a heart
It slithered into your pocket
The smaller one
The one we wonder of
What's the purpose
My love is roughly
The size of a quarter
Stuffed in your pocket
But if you don't spend it
If you invest it
Back into me
It'll grow like a tree
It'll tower over us both
With fruit we can eat
But I can see you
Eyeing those machines
To get a figurine
Or cheap plastic ring
And you'll present it to me...

<table>
<tr><td>Patient Name:
JOHN QUEOR</td><td></td><td>Procedure: BYPASS</td></tr>
<tr><td>Page: 117</td><td></td><td>I WILL ALWAYS LEAVE
(CONT.)</td></tr>
</table>

...

And I'll leave

I'll blow more rings

I'll feed the machines

I will always leave

If I were   A Flower   And
You were A   Bee
I would Fall   Like A Tree   Wishing
You'd Land on Me
But If You Did
I would Die
The moment You Left
To Return
To
The Hive
15

<table>
<tr><td>Patient Name:
  JOHN QUEOR</td><td></td><td>Procedure: BYPASS</td></tr>
<tr><td>Page: 119</td><td></td><td>**SHATTER**</td></tr>
</table>

Shards on the kitchen floor
Like leaves emancipated
To pile and be raked away
I wanted to pick them up
Glue it all back together
I wanted to cry for a while
Glue it all back together
I wanted to find numbness
Collect myself in a dustpan
Discard myself into the trash can
I can't keep everything whole
I do not own gravity
Things come and they go
Porcelain sometimes explodes
Into a small constellation
That at some point
Must be let go of

<table>
<tr><td>Patient Name:
JOHN QUEOR</td><td></td><td>Procedure: BYPASS</td></tr>
<tr><td>Page: 120</td><td></td><td>**DNR**</td></tr>
</table>

If ever

The rest

Of my hope

Dies

DNR

I've been

Running

In circles

Digging

A trench

Or

Is it

A grave

Either way

If ever

The rest

Of my hope

Dies

DNR

It's immense
But it's mine
I really don't mind
The throbbing
The wallowing
The wondering
The way I conceal
Camouflage
Smile
Slip forward
Knowing
No matter what
I'll always feel this
And it's immense
But it's mine
So I don't mind

<table>
<tr><td>Patient Name:
JOHN QUEOR</td><td></td><td>Procedure: BYPASS</td></tr>
<tr><td>Page: 122</td><td></td><td>LOVE BALM</td></tr>
</table>

Deceptive poison kiss
I store you in a bottle
I rub you on my lips
Pinot noir spill stain
I'm going insane
Ogling intensely
You are acid rain

Deer in the headlights
You accelerate
Dent in your hood
Dead in the road

Curse the wind
You breathe deeply
Caress your face
To scratch your cheek
And enchant your lips
With Pinot Noir stained
Poison kiss

John Queor

Valentine

When love pours down
I open my umbrella
I crawl inside of myself
I search for shelter

I don't want to catch a cold
From standing there soaking
Waiting for the praise to sour
To circle back to my mistakes

When love pours down
I wrap myself in cellophane
I'll absolutely asphyxiate
One way or another

<table>
<tr><td>Patient Name:
  JOHN QUEOR</td><td></td><td>Procedure: BYPASS</td></tr>
<tr><td>Page: 125</td><td></td><td>I CAN'T HELP THAT I
LIKE THEM CRAZY</td></tr>
</table>

I can't help that I like them crazy
Cradle his crises like my baby
Manic running in light-year circles
Forgetting about the walls approaching
When he hits it's always so hard
Crumbling to the floor slow motion
Leaving a mess wherever he relaxes
But I loved him most in those moments
A hummingbird finally perching
The unobtainable suddenly obtained
Until morning came and he was new
A fresh and wild fire burning
And I returned back into my blue
To bask and repeat a few times more
Until he stopped knocking at the door

*Author's Note: This poem is not about physical violence. It instead refers to how fast the mood can change, leaving you with the feeling of being hit. If you do find yourself relating to this poem in terms of physical violence, please speak up and call the **Domestic Violence Hotline** at 800-799-7233.

There are days
Where I feel invisible
Like no one in the world
Has ever gazed upon me
It's comforting
To be unknown
Alone
To breathe
Without anyone
Asking why
And not knowing
How
To answer

<table>
<tr><td>Patient Name:
  JOHN QUEOR</td><td></td><td>Procedure: BYPASS</td></tr>
<tr><td>Page: 127</td><td></td><td>AND THEN I DID</td></tr>
</table>

I was at the white part
Curling under myself
Spiraling and crashing
Into bubbles on the beach
The sky was green
Politely taunting me
Resting on top of me
Crashing onto me
It was actively falling
And I couldn't catch it
I've never wanted to fly
Gravity is kind to me
But I've always wanted
To implode
I think you taught me how to
I was staring out the window once
Wondering how I could get away
Without drowning
And then I did

<table>
<tr><td>Patient Name:
  JOHN QUEOR</td><td></td><td>Procedure: BYPASS</td></tr>
<tr><td>Page: 128</td><td></td><td>I USED TO</td></tr>
</table>

I used to see pictures in dancing flame
I used to dance on empty streets
Before living through the photographs
Before drinking through all my pain
Stargazing standing at the crossroads
Stargazing with the misfit kids
Waiting for a grand moment to find me
Waiting alone by the cellphone glow
Longing for a life different than mine
Longing to be entangled in a web
Smiling as the snow piled around me
Smiling as the snow turned into bloom
Promising a better year was coming
Promising myself that I could change
Salutations to all the ghosts behind me
Salutations to the child still inside me
I see new horizons amongst the rubble
I see my reflection without a wince
I used to see pictures in dancing flame
I used to dance on empty streets

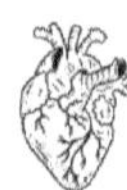

<table>
<tr><td>Patient Name:
JOHN QUEOR</td><td></td><td>Procedure: BYPASS</td></tr>
<tr><td>Page: 129</td><td></td><td>FRACTION</td></tr>
</table>

It's just skin and bones
Periodic fluctuations
You could set up camp
Make your home here
When the time comes
For you to rest your hand
On my high shoulders
Or the small of my back
Wrap me in your arms
Hold me tightly
While stars explode
And we can go
We could go home
As a perfect fit
A matching set
One single soul
Just cut in half

Maybe we could take a stroll
Upon crisp brown and orange
Leaves cascading around us
Like we're two figurines inside
A glass ball lightly shaken

And I can help you with your dreams
And you can teach me to be more open
And I won't be uncomfortable
When you touch me

We can sit beneath a tree
Completely quiet while we watch
Ripples dance across the pond
You'll look at me and yawn
And I'll let you stretch upon me
Like a leaf on the water
We could drift off together

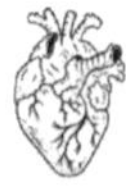

<table>
<tr><td>Patient Name:
  JOHN QUEOR</td><td></td><td>Procedure: BYPASS</td></tr>
<tr><td>Page: 133</td><td></td><td>**YOUNG LOVE**</td></tr>
</table>

Young love

Has stripes of silver

And a layer of lotion

Over the fine lines

Growing under the eyes

Sometimes

It wakes up to back pain

And fading memories

Of kissing beneath the stars

And speeding down the highway

While the birth of two dreams

Combined

And then dissolved

On the tongue

Like spun sugar

<table>
<tr><td>Patient Name:
  JOHN QUEOR</td><td></td><td>Procedure: BYPASS</td></tr>
<tr><td>Page: 134</td><td></td><td>BARTON'S</td></tr>
</table>

Not very long after meeting
We let the substances steal us both away
I clung onto the stopper of the drain
You let go and almost swirled the rest of the way
I wouldn't know anything about you anymore
Just the wild times we chaotically shared
I wanted to call you a little while ago
But I know better than to open that gate
Wrapped in spikes to slam in my face
You taught me about another kind of love
Our souls were shards of the same piece
Just destined to go in separate directions
I'd love to go back for a little while
Chase our Barton's with cans of Dole
Lounge on your couch for days at a time
When the world was comfortably passing us by
But in those moments we were fine
Young, stupid, crazy, alive

What if I wasn't longing alone
And you too felt something for me
It's the oldest story in the book
Boy falls for boy who falls for girl
But maybe this one will be different
A sun that doesn't destroy my wings
Catching my gaze and returning one
Softly inviting me to pursue
To climb into your cherry eyes
And peruse your thoughts collecting
A deep nervousness like mine
I'll move slow and walk the line
But only if I'm not longing alone

<table>
<tr><td>Patient Name:
  JOHN QUEOR</td><td></td><td>Procedure: BYPASS</td></tr>
<tr><td>Page: 136</td><td></td><td>**SACCHARINE**</td></tr>
</table>

Milk and honey

Smooth and sweet

To be caressed

By the rough

Calloused fingertips

Exploring

I am soft vanilla

But so cold

Like ice cream

To melt

Glistening on

Your bottom lip

To be licked

Like

Milk and honey

<table>
<tr><td>Patient Name:
JOHN QUEOR</td><td></td><td>Procedure: BYPASS</td></tr>
<tr><td>Page: 137</td><td></td><td>**CONNECTION**</td></tr>
</table>

Take me to your paradise
The soft noises escaping
Like breath but boisterous
Slowly rising and falling
With eyes falling on mine

You can be my youth fountain
Fix what was broken the last time
I was sprawled beneath a body
That lasted far beyond the sell date

I'll take you to my paradise
All the curves and pressure points
Teeth to make soft impressions
As fireworks light up our sky
And we stay connected in the moment

I live in a constant state of fear
That if things are going too well
My life will immediately cease
And I'll be stuffed in a pine box
To rot and be forgotten about

I find myself feeling blessed
When something spills or breaks
Because then I'm able to breathe
And continue to occupy this space

And when my heart is broken
Happy tears dance down my face
As I exist in an emotional duality
Resting within the spill between
The soft air and angry sea

<table>
<tr><td>Patient Name:
JOHN QUEOR</td><td></td><td>Procedure: BYPASS</td></tr>
<tr><td>Page: 139</td><td></td><td>**OPEN HEART**</td></tr>
</table>

My heart
Is more open
In the dark

It knows best
The chill of
Midnight breaths

I exhale alongside
Such a long sigh
Because I am in love

With the solitude

Some days
I have no idea
How to continue
To ask the divine
To give me strength
To give me
Another person
To portray
I can't be me today
Who was I
Yesterday
The day before
I don't feel present
I'm in the closet
In a basement
On the moon
The side that
The sun isn't
Kissing

<table>
<tr><td>Patient Name:
JOHN QUEOR</td><td></td><td>Procedure: BYPASS</td></tr>
<tr><td>Page: 141</td><td></td><td>CURTAINS</td></tr>
</table>

How many lives
Can I fit into this one
Can I reincarnate
Even prior to passing
Who else can I be
Where can I go
Who will fall behind me
Or trailblaze so fast ahead
Maybe I'll know you again
Maybe you'll forget me
Or watch me explode
Could you hold me
Like a Fourth of July
Sparkler in the night
Without getting burned
And still be able to catch
My wild fascination
How many lives
Can I fit into this one
Who will still be beside me
When the curtains close

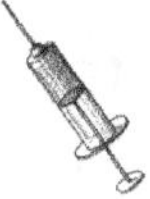

It was devastating
Watching my teenage dream
Suffocate inside of me
My darkest thoughts
Reminding me
I was never good enough
To be held the way I hoped
Or kissed the way I saw
On the television screen

I have never not been discarded
I have never *not* sabotaged myself
I let all of these years escape me
Forgetting that I couldn't go back
I wasted so much time hating myself
I wasted so much time drowning myself...

<table>
<tr><td>Patient Name:
  JOHN QUEOR</td><td></td><td>Procedure: BYPASS</td></tr>
<tr><td>Page: 143</td><td></td><td>TELEVISION (CONT.)</td></tr>
</table>

...

It was devastating

Watching my teenage dream

Suffocate inside of me

But I still have time

To be wrapped in arms

And covered in kisses

The ways I've seen

On the television screens

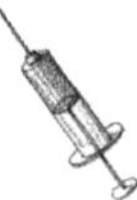

I know you're out there
Gazing into the gray void
A cloudy starless sky
Waiting for your dreams to ignite
To part from your pure soul
To finally cross paths with mine
You can dance on all of my pages
The blank white I pepper with thoughts
Maybe you're a painter
I could be the froth of the sea
Perhaps you are a musician
I could get lost in your symphony
Maybe you're a dreamer
I could rest my head on your chest
To go on beautiful journeys with you
Maybe I'm writing this to myself
Maybe I'm writing this to the past
Maybe I'm writing this to you
A soul I've still yet to know
Watching the sky all alone

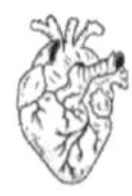

4.11.23

Will I be aware when
the gold begins to descend
Upon my crown of shadows
How will I feel when I know
that some stars have returned
as light to soothe my darkness
While the rest of me is out exploring
how to smooth out the rough ends
frayed by forces of Jagged nature
who didn't know they were cruel
Gilded honey come drizzle down
Upon what I keep beneath my crown

I'd banish all of my possessions
To rest my face against your chest
Absorbing your sweet heart beating
Like a criminal cracking a safe
Once open I wouldn't take a thing
Just polish what was hidden away
And marvel at the museum
Relaxing beautifully beside me

After sharing with you my flame
I'd kiss your forehead and go away
Because to thine own self be true
And I only really crave the blue

I'd tuck your photo in my soul
Which has become quite the portfolio
Smiles to illuminate my sky
When I too find myself lost
And I wouldn't mind being lost with you
For a brief moment to fully unleash you
And slink off before the sun rises
To encounter someone else like you

<table>
<tr><td>Patient Name:
JOHN QUEOR</td><td></td><td>Procedure: BYPASS</td></tr>
<tr><td>Page: 147</td><td></td><td>ROSE WATER</td></tr>
</table>

I presented a bouquet of roses
Hiding all the thorns under my tongue
My lips were rouged from blood
I wouldn't let slip from the corners

Life isn't smooth
It's not meant to be
The most beautiful things
Are better off seen
And let be
But we fall
And it stings
And we cry
And we sing

Or write poetry
About love that was given
But just couldn't be absorbed
No matter how many nights
I dreamed to obtain it

All I've ever wanted was love
And when I'm ready
I'll let myself have it

I've entertained the wrong vibrations
Happy just to have felt something
Knowing there was greater out there
Waiting for me to realize I'm worthy
And throw myself into the fire
Where I burn without the hurt

All I've ever wanted was love
And when I'm ready
I'll let you have it

<table>
<tr><td>Patient Name:
  JOHN QUEOR</td><td></td><td>Procedure: BYPASS</td></tr>
<tr><td>Page: 149</td><td></td><td>**SMILE LINES**</td></tr>
</table>

I recall my old dreams
You would be in love with me
It's kind of funny now I guess
Because I never could love myself
Kind of cruel to expect that of you
But I would have saturated you
I think in silly ways I still do
I talk with the universe about you
Hoping all of your dreams bloom
Flourishing like a butterfly garden
Delicate wings like your eyes
They had the same sadness as mine
I hope you have smile lines
I hope yours go deeper than mine
It's kind of funny now I guess

HOW CAN I
168043
Hold on to
myself
while
Also
Letting it all go

<table>
<tr><td>Patient Name:
  JOHN QUEOR</td><td></td><td>Procedure: BYPASS</td></tr>
<tr><td>Page: 151</td><td></td><td>AVEC MOI</td></tr>
</table>

Fall into my grasp
Lie *avec moi* on the sweet grass
Drink the August haze with me
Condensation slipping
Moisture trailing downward
How many stars are above
Could you find love in me
Could you fall endlessly
Mutually orbiting one another
Show me your sherbet sunrise
Wrap me in your vengeful tides
Lie *avec moi* on the sunned sand
Nothing to give
Nothing to take
Mutually orbiting

Avec moi: French for 'with me'

<table>
<tr><td>Patient Name:
  JOHN QUEOR</td><td></td><td>Procedure: BYPASS</td></tr>
<tr><td>Page: 152</td><td></td><td>MY LOVE</td></tr>
</table>

My love is static
Little specks
Of gray and white
And black
Electric
Underwhelming
Overwhelming
Complex yet
Simple
Given
Exhausted
Taken away
My love is static
It travels
Everywhere
It goes
Further than I can
Could you imagine
How clear things will be
When it is received
Broadcasted
In his eyes
And I finally see the same

I was hypnotized by
Your cigarette swirls
The way I couldn't have you
The ways that I could
Sprawled out together
Like freshly dried laundry
Thrown so haphazardly
Atop a freshly made bed
Releasing our clouds
To be dazed in a haze
I watched myself
From across the room
Accidentally fall for you
I knew it would end terribly
Two trains on one track
Heading towards one another
I've spent most of my life ruined
And yet I still can't look away
From the falling debris

<table>
<tr><td>Patient Name:
  JOHN QUEOR</td><td></td><td>Procedure: BYPASS</td></tr>
<tr><td>Page: 154</td><td></td><td>**PROPOFOL**</td></tr>
</table>

I want a lover

Like propofol

Send me

To slumber

To rest

For hours

In his craters

Waking

Ready

To go back

To sleep

I'm tired

More so

Than ever

Administer the

Medicated kiss

Cradle me

While I crash

Still touching

Your lips

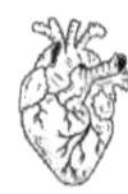

Horizontal...
      your earring glistening
in the candle light...
      hesitation
what would you do
if I ran my tongue
      slowly up your neck
pulling that earring
            with my teeth...
      wine glasses resting.
      a bottle fully split
and the candle
            flickers along

a gift of words to be used.

<table>
<tr><td>Patient Name:
JOHN QUEOR</td><td></td><td>Procedure: BYPASS</td></tr>
<tr><td>Page: 156</td><td></td><td>SAHARA</td></tr>
</table>

Love
Did you ever loathe to hold me
Was I very
Much
Like a desert
That
Not even you
Could moisturize

There's a puncture in this vessel
That once loved so ferociously
It bleeds out so fast like lightning
And there just isn't a patch
Or suture or glue or staple
That can close this wound

The sun rises each morning
And breath is dragged inside
And I'm beside you and elated
Nervous and completely satiated
But caught in a whirlwind of wonder
As to if I'm giving you enough

There's a puncture in this vessel
That caused me to feel so numb
These arteries hardened so fast
Never expecting to feel loved again
But the sun rose one morning
And the air tasted like honey roses

<table>
<tr><td>Patient Name:
  JOHN QUEOR</td><td></td><td>Procedure: BYPASS</td></tr>
<tr><td>Page: 158</td><td></td><td>**ENUNCIATION**</td></tr>
</table>

I wish I were your lip balm
To glide across those dusty rose
Pillows resting on your face
Pursed and speaking gently
Of something I have no clue
Because my eyes are glued
On the twists and curves
Syllables and alliteration
Feeling the passionate punctuation
And then you smile and I wished
Your teeth were crooked
So I could be your braces
And then I wished that you were naked
So I could be your clothes
And then I wished the Earth was destroyed
So that I could be your home

<table>
<tr><td>Patient Name:
JOHN QUEOR</td><td></td><td>Procedure: BYPASS</td></tr>
<tr><td>Page: 159</td><td></td><td>DENIM</td></tr>
</table>

If there's space inside
I'd love if I could occupy

Two patches just waiting
To be sewn to a denim jacket
Perhaps side by side
Fibers barely touching

I'd be happy to be your company
A soft gust crossing our frays
Growing into gentle brush strokes
Sunlight setting your eyes on fire
An amber glow that offers warmth

If there's space inside
I'd very much like to occupy

Destroy that vacancy sign
And turn your heart into home
Just two patches who
Finally found their jacket

<table>
<tr><td>Patient Name:
  JOHN QUEOR</td><td></td><td>Procedure: BYPASS</td></tr>
<tr><td>Page: 161</td><td></td><td>**POETRY IS MY
BOYFRIEND**</td></tr>
</table>

Poetry is my boyfriend
He kisses me at sunrise
While I'm still dreaming
Caught up in the stars
For us to connect the dots
When inspiration knocks
And he's naked on my bed
Face down and ass up
I scribble lines on his back
And rehearse them
Then I photograph him
We climax together
And I light him a cigarette
As he wipes my tears
And hums me a lullaby
And then kisses me at sunrise
While I'm still dreaming

<table>
<tr><td>Patient Name:
JOHN QUEOR</td><td></td><td>Procedure: BYPASS</td></tr>
<tr><td>Page: 162</td><td></td><td>BYPASS III.</td></tr>
</table>

I was never foolish
To continue falling
After healing

I can suffer

I was never foolish
To continue giving
After I was gone

I can see

I was never honest
Of what I needed
When I needed

I can need

<table>
<tr><td>Patient Name:
  JOHN QUEOR</td><td></td><td>Procedure: BYPASS</td></tr>
<tr><td>Page: 164</td><td></td><td>MIDSUMMER</td></tr>
</table>

I returned to the peak
We had climbed
You sat in the gravel
Letting the sun fall
On your skin gently
Like a butterfly
Perching on a flower
I can't describe
The exact feeling
I felt
When deception
Fell on me like fallout
Staining my skin green
And burning my eyes
Confirming all I felt
That has followed me
To everyone else
Corroding my heart

Don't ever let me go
We sang surrounded by roses
During candlelit waltzes
But who's at fault

It fizzles away, baby
Nothing gold can stay
Winter melts to May
And candles waltz

Pricked by the roses
Pricked by the boy
And then it melts away
It all just goes away

<table>
<tr><td>Patient Name:
  JOHN QUEOR</td><td></td><td>Procedure: BYPASS</td></tr>
<tr><td>Page: 166</td><td></td><td>A STAR I CAST
MY GAZE UPON</td></tr>
</table>

There are lines on the face of your surface
And pollution dissipating in your core
Free as the air you meander for miles
Free as the air you cannot be kept
Your rivers run clean and clear
Babbling for days sometimes rapidly
I looked directly into the sun
It saturated you causing a shimmer
To form on your highest point
Sometimes I feel completely mad
Alone in an ever-changing labyrinth
I think I might be Mars
You are actually closer to the sun
You share your warmth in crazy waves
I'm much colder in some ways
There are lines on the face of your surface
I'll never be the sun or moon
I'm content as an admirer

<table>
<tr><td>Patient Name:
  JOHN QUEOR</td><td></td><td>Procedure: BYPASS</td></tr>
<tr><td>Page: 167</td><td></td><td>LINGER LONGER</td></tr>
</table>

My whole world is a minefield
There's eggshells everywhere
And it makes me so uncomfortable
Letting you know I'm uncomfortable
So I linger for a little longer waiting
For my spine to get a little stronger
And my heart to get a little more numb
There's broken glass in the kitchen
Where we used to drink dark liquor
And dance to the slow and sad songs
I used to write love poetry to while
The sun climbed into our eyes smiling
And now my feet are bleeding and
You are smiling with your shoes on
And I would just really like to cry
But my eyes continuously stay dry

<table>
<tr><td>Patient Name:
JOHN QUEOR</td><td></td><td>Procedure: BYPASS</td></tr>
<tr><td>Page: 169</td><td></td><td>I KEEP WAITING</td></tr>
</table>

I keep waiting
For the sun to spill
Over the horizon
Illuminating
A single path
Of ten thousand
Dandelions
Tickled by
My breath
Joined with
The breeze
To push the seeds
Like snow upon
My waking dream
Walking towards me
In a field of weeds
Just in time for
The roses to
Bloom

<table>
<tr><td>Patient Name:
  JOHN QUEOR</td><td></td><td>Procedure: BYPASS</td></tr>
<tr><td>Page: 170</td><td></td><td>ONE NIGHT</td></tr>
</table>

Wear my happy tears on your pulse points
Submerge me into your youth fountain
I just want to be wild for you tonight
I want to scream into the void with you
Knees sinking on a black comforter
Anoint my third eye with ylang-ylang
As wisps of lemongrass take me to summer
Drift away on moon-kissed cloud shapes
Touch me with only your soft exhales
Draw your favorite flower on my back
And I'll describe to you my own heaven
Candles flickering with your tongue
To decipher whether I am to be
Considered sweet or if I am savory
And I'll hold tightly onto the moment
Laughing and mental-photographing
Because once the sun breaks the horizon
I'll leave and never come back again

<table>
<tr><td>Patient Name:
  JOHN QUEOR</td><td></td><td>Procedure: BYPASS</td></tr>
<tr><td>Page: 171</td><td></td><td>HEART-SHAPED LOCKET</td></tr>
</table>

Bury yourself in my heart-shaped locket
We can sit at the bay window together
Watching the world implode around us
But while we wait we can explore
Place your hands against my rose hips
Taste the peppermint chill on my lips
You could lie me down on the lemongrass
Cinnamon and ginger exploding
I gift to you this bouquet of jasmine
The fire is crackling we can burn
We can steep on the loveseat
You can be my wild chamomile
Exhaust me and send me to sleep
Where I could dream of a world
Where this didn't have to end
But I can smell the smoke thicken
We're only moments away
From notes of pine and bitter char
But
You'll be safe here
In my heart-shaped locket

<table>
<tr><td>Patient Name:
  JOHN QUEOR</td><td></td><td>Procedure: BYPASS</td></tr>
<tr><td>Page: 172</td><td></td><td>WET</td></tr>
</table>

Show me those sparkling bedroom eyes
Sultry and twisted wearing a smile
And I so quickly fall inside
The neon lit catacombs
Where our minds collide
And I can feel the thunder
Lightning not so far behind
I want to be caught in the vines
Vibrant flower and thorns are sweet
Evaporating from your heat
Transforming into drops of dew
Osmosis meandering to saturate you

<table>
<tr><td>Patient Name:
  JOHN QUEOR</td><td></td><td>Procedure: BYPASS</td></tr>
<tr><td>Page: 173</td><td></td><td>DAYDREAM</td></tr>
</table>

His hair was like tilled earth
Softly drizzled in honey
His eyes were much the same
I never caught his name
But that didn't stop me
From taking time to imagine
His breath on my neck
Embracing to depart
In the snow on our first date
A quiet little coffee house
That we brought to life
With laughter and stories
Quick holding of hands
Brushing the hair away
That hid the melted honey
Mouths tasting of coffee
His hair was like tilled earth
His eyes were much the same
I never caught his name

There are cracks in the cement
I feel the tears turn into spheres
To leak down my rusted cheeks
I feel too shocked to speak
Frozen in place and hoping
Someone can fix the fracture
Before the earth has time to open
Like Parisian doors holding back a storm
I can feel the protons charging
They will soon deeply kiss the sky
And tear open all of my time capsules
Releasing the pain that
I was saving for later
In Chinese takeaway boxes
Stored in the back of the fridge

I was completely satiated
Until the fractures turned into breaks

I never imagined I'd encounter
All these goodbyes collecting
Like butterflies in a mesh net
To escape and return to haunt me
Reminding me of exactly who I am
And the processes of transformation
I was made to undergo
My seams are all sealed in gold
As I sit beneath a willow tree
And offer tears of my own
To all of those
With and beyond me
That I had to release
To forge a path adjacent to me
My love is a gift that you can keep
But it will not be replenished
If ever you forget or waste it

<table>
<tr><td>Patient Name:
  JOHN QUEOR</td><td></td><td>Procedure: BYPASS</td></tr>
<tr><td>Page: 176</td><td></td><td>**SMOLDERING**</td></tr>
</table>

I wish I could still utilize
Your arms to tether me here
Gravity is loosening it's grip
And I fear soon I'll float free
Up and right into the sun

At that point I would've been
Burned in every possible way
Not even ashes left behind
For you to add to your shrine
Realizing I was your philosophy

Now ether to slowly seep across
And into those pensive eyes
Questioning and wondering
What could have been
And who I did become

9.24.23

I'll slowdance again in the warmth
of swaying light on the walls in the living room
I'll laugh until the sun slides through the window
and then I'll slide between the sheets and
yawn as an arm wraps around me slowly
I'm working harder on myself this time
maybe in two years I'll let you chase me
into the field that used to be corn
into my dreams swirling the sun with the stars
into my heart caught with my head in the clouds
into my palms where I'll spread a wish with a whisper
I'm more sun-kissed this time around
my battles won't bring you down when you come
from behind the veil the gods hid you behind
in wait for the final edit of me to emerge
when the lightning finally causes a surge

<table>
<tr><td>Patient Name:
  JOHN QUEOR</td><td></td><td>Procedure: BYPASS</td></tr>
<tr><td>Page: 178</td><td></td><td>***NOSOTROS***</td></tr>
</table>

When you come this time
I'll be prepared
To draw my lines
To sprawl upon you
To whisper my dreams
Into the air we share
Our moments are fleeting
I'll be torn from here soon
I feel your shadow
I see it before I sleep
We are two circles
That when combined
Make infinity
When you come this time
I'll dissolve into you
I'll burn like the sun
I'll feel your friction
Your hand on my face
Breathing sweet words
Into the air we share

Nosotros: Spanish for 'us'

<table>
<tr><td>Patient Name:
JOHN QUEOR</td><td></td><td>Procedure: BYPASS</td></tr>
<tr><td>Page: 179</td><td></td><td>LA PETITE MORT</td></tr>
</table>

Took myself into Nirvana
Matters into my own hand
Visuals behind shut eyes
Your skin sparkled aspirated
Into your little death

Eager eyes
Sultry descent
Pale Adonis

Took you into Nirvana
Golden ticket plus one
Hot honey drizzle down
From heaven into my mouth
Into our little death

<table>
<tr><td>Patient Name:
JOHN QUEOR</td><td></td><td>Procedure: BYPASS</td></tr>
<tr><td>Page: 180</td><td></td><td>WATERWAYS</td></tr>
</table>

These rivers could lead me
To whichever sea you reside
To the sandy bottom floor
Where you've chosen to hide
Perhaps incredibly soon
I'll have swam down to your side
And we can emerge together
From the depths to the tides

My hope is endless
Like the stars and sun
Fragments of light
Reflecting from the sea
Where I know you are
Down there waiting for me

These rivers will lead me
To your pearlescent shining eyes
As I wait for you endlessly
Under an ever-changing sky

<table>
<tr><td>Patient Name:
  JOHN QUEOR</td><td></td><td>Procedure: BYPASS</td></tr>
<tr><td>Page: 181</td><td></td><td>LOVESICK</td></tr>
</table>

I'm homesick for a heart

I'm not quite sure

Exists for me

I know I'll learn

To be without

To live without

I've been practicing

For many moons now

JIM
NANCY

<table>
<tr><td>Patient Name:
JOHN QUEOR</td><td></td><td>Procedure: BYPASS</td></tr>
<tr><td>Page: 183</td><td></td><td>LIKE CLIMBING ROSES</td></tr>
</table>

Could you be my paradise
Might I lounge upon you
Drape myself so gently
Over your skin like silk
Perhaps you could love me
Drape yourself over me
Upon each one of my bones
If you could be my paradise
I could be your home
Etch our initials
Deeply in the foundation
As was done in
The house I grew up in
Encircled in a heart
Traced over whenever
If ever
We forget how precious
It is to be in paradise
And to have a home
And these bones
That twist to hold
Like climbing roses

<table>
<tr><td>Patient Name:
  JOHN QUEOR</td><td></td><td>Procedure: BYPASS</td></tr>
<tr><td>Page: 184</td><td></td><td>BIOLOGY</td></tr>
</table>

Friction of index and middle finger
Dragging gently over lips and chin
With pupils fixated on tongue and teeth
Breath slowly exiting our soft temples
Eyelids flutter closed for quick moments
Of glimpses into our personal Nirvana

Teeth pressed into flesh
I want my head on your chest
Fingers twirling in my hair
Our particles are everywhere

Friction of hand closed over throat
Squeezing and in some time releasing
With irises diving deep in mine glowing
Smile bursting from sinister tempting
And soon your fingers will be in my hair
Our particles spread out everywhere

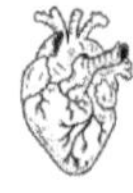

I can still smell the vanilla sugar
Clinging to your colorless frame
That also thankfully clung to mine
You were an awakening to me
A different life that felt more like mine
Not the cookie cutout I was living
Everything smelled like fresh rain
The kind that comes at night
Cool on the skin in the summer
Pairs well with the vanilla sugar
I was so thankful to have met you
As we drifted to different corners
I tried to find that body spray on eBay
It's been discontinued for a while now
I bounce between the now and then
Sitting in the center of infinity

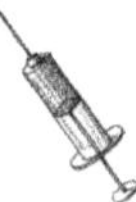

<table>
<tr><td>Patient Name:
  JOHN QUEOR</td><td></td><td>Procedure: BYPASS</td></tr>
<tr><td>Page: 186</td><td></td><td>**STAND**</td></tr>
</table>

Comfortable rectangle
Entanglements
Stranger sleeping
Feeling, breathing
Mostly dreaming

Sinful exploration
Starlit touching
Skin cells
Sweet nothings
Strands of hair

Morning whispers
Morning breath
Laughing, touching
Alarm clocks
Departures

<table>
<tr><td>Patient Name:
JOHN QUEOR</td><td></td><td>Procedure: BYPASS</td></tr>
<tr><td>Page: 187</td><td></td><td>AURORA BOREALIS</td></tr>
</table>

I'm choked out
By the ghost
Of a man
Who never
Laid a single
Finger on me

He looked into my eyes
Our breaths funneled into one
A cyclone of silly dreams
But only on one side

I've searched
A hundred skies
To find my own
Aurora borealis
He never looked back
Into my eyes

The lack of a glance back
Made it burn a little better
I really only ever want
That which will never want me...

...

In those searing
Moments escaping
My skies are painted
Green and pale blue
Aurora borealis

<table>
<tr><td>Patient Name:
  JOHN QUEOR</td><td></td><td>Procedure: BYPASS</td></tr>
<tr><td>Page: 189</td><td></td><td>JEFF</td></tr>
</table>

Pale blue button up
Not buttoned up
Wild red wood falling
Tucked back
Behind your ears
As harmonies escape
Through your lips
And moving fingertips
High notes levitating
Right at eye level
You look through me
I am glass
So it makes sense
You're behind it
And you're singing
Beautifully
Forever
Beautifully

Ascending alongside the temperature
The sun feels so close even at night
A mirage spreading out on my mattress
Opalescent glimmers like sweat beads
Fingers stretching out to brush against
Skin blistering beneath the dream catcher
Where will you be when I wake up
Will I visit you when your fever begins
To dab a cool cloth on your brow
To whisper stories of love
To break away as dawn begins
As the perspiration evaporates
To slip back to 98.6°

<table>
<tr><td>Patient Name:
JOHN QUEOR</td><td></td><td>Procedure: BYPASS</td></tr>
<tr><td>Page: 192</td><td></td><td>**DNA**</td></tr>
</table>

I'll perfect the flesh
But
You still won't want me
It's not a matter
Of skin stretched
To cover the muscle or
The frame lying within me
It goes deeper
To the cells that decided
My room would be deep blue
Decorated with lions and grenades
I love being blue
But I can't ignore
The pink that shines through
It's just not quite bright enough
To fascinate
To distract from the disturbance
The ropes that twist inside me
Are crystal clear to me
But I get
How it could get
Confusing

<table>
<tr><td>Patient Name:
  JOHN QUEOR</td><td></td><td>Procedure: BYPASS</td></tr>
<tr><td>Page: 193</td><td></td><td>**FLUSHED**</td></tr>
</table>

I held you

Respectfully

My world was dying

It was black

And green

Flaking away

Like a skin disease

But when

I was connected

To you

My world was

Porcelain pink

Flushed

Spring roses

My elation was foolish

No garden survives

Winter dandruff

<table>
<tr><td>Patient Name:
  JOHN QUEOR</td><td></td><td>Procedure: BYPASS</td></tr>
<tr><td>Page: 194</td><td></td><td>**ROSE HIPS**</td></tr>
</table>

I let my walls crumble
I immediately rebuilt
With stronger material
If ever I needed you
That was last year
Spring came and went
My seeds didn't sprout
The trees are shedding
I still sometimes dream
Quietly
Grayscale
Far away

I felt a shift in my existence
Everything is different now
There's a hole in my stomach
Where the butterflies roamed
They have all escaped from me
The moths have fled me as well
There's no name for how I feel
I know the clouds are coming
I feel a need to rush for cover
I don't know if I'll survive this alone
But I've come this far
And I'm going further
With or without you

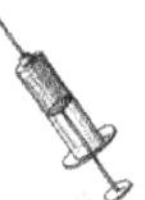

Love to me is a hummingbird
A rare sight to be enjoyed
For longer than a second
I feel like I'm floating too
But kind of like an old balloon
My string is rubbing the pavement
Aren't we all searching for sugar
Wishing a moment could last forever
Wishing one promise would prevail
But who would I be as two now
I keep my grocery bags
In the passenger seat
I come and go wherever
Whenever I please
I sleep in the center of the bed
I spread upon it for miles
I spill over the sides
Like warm ganache upon a cake
And I collect myself when I wake
Like hair pulled into a messy bun
To throw on a shirt and pants and run
Wherever the wind commands
I hate to say it
But one is grand

<table>
<tr><td>Patient Name:
JOHN QUEOR</td><td></td><td>Procedure: BYPASS</td></tr>
<tr><td>Page: 197</td><td></td><td>GOLDEN GAZE</td></tr>
</table>

I hope his eyes are golden
Like a fall leaf preserved in amber
Held in July afternoon sunlight
I hope they stream beams of
Soft iridescent flashes
To sway on my exposed skin
To sink into me like moisturizer
To replenish what was taken
I've seen blue for so long
Small aggressive oceans
And moss covered boulders
Even the icebergs have the hue
I once had a peppermint gaze
Fall upon me like stage lights
There was a malfunction somehow
With the cords to the curtains
Causing a year long encore
We exited the stage separate ways
I took a breath and locked the gate
But I'm feeling ready to emerge
To stretch and fall into the earth
Caught in a golden gaze

My heart is full
That is wealth
It expands
And contracts
That is science

I hold on
For too long
It solidifies
Into a blockage

I'll be better
After the bypass
I will expand again
And then contract
That is nature

<table>
<tr><td>Patient Name:
  JOHN QUEOR</td><td></td><td>Procedure: BYPASS</td></tr>
<tr><td>Page: 200</td><td></td><td>SEASIDE DREAM</td></tr>
</table>

I often entertain the idea of change
Fleeing this town to be near the ocean
Starting fresh before my hair is white
A youthful sparkle still in my eyes I'll
Build something incredibly beautiful
From weathered bricks and rubble
With the sea as my backsplash
A small cottage on the coast
Candles dancing day and night
I'll walk in the fall air
Into the town square
To peruse the market isles
I'll notice I'm being noticed
He'll notice that I notice
Small conversations will turn to
Sparkling water on the shore
He'll fight to get to know me
And one day I'll let him in
And he'll gesture for my hand
And one day I'll let him win
The sea as our backsplash
A small cottage on the coast
Our hair completely white
Our eyes a youthful sparkle

In loving memory of Ann Bitterman

<table>
<tr><td>Patient Name:
JOHN QUEOR</td><td></td><td>Procedure: BYPASS</td></tr>
<tr><td>Page: 203</td><td></td><td>MY BROTHERS</td></tr>
</table>

Jacob once left early in the morning
Hours after my heart was turned
Into cement and then crushed dust
To take home the one responsible
So I wouldn't have to worry when I woke
Jordan always stood a little further back
But always had a severity to him like a snake
Not in a bad way if you were on his good side
I often crossed that line when we were young
And he always made it a point to keep me aware
But when the matter would get out of hand
Just like the air he would be there
We differ in extraordinary ways
But we're also all very much the same
And I'm so grateful that I have them
Best friends with built-in lenses
Who can find me when I blend in
With the night sky like a new moon
I dedicate a quadrant for them alone

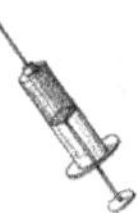

<table>
<tr><td>Patient Name:
JOHN QUEOR</td><td></td><td>Procedure: BYPASS</td></tr>
<tr><td>Page: 204</td><td></td><td>JANE ELAINE</td></tr>
</table>

I inherited my love
For the twinkle of the city
And the divine power
Of femininity
From my grandmother
Who chose
Somewhere in the middle
That she didn't have to settle
And that inspires me
She always gets things done
Elegantly and effortlessly
And I take that into myself
She's exactly five feet
But light-years deep
With love that she showers
Forever over her family

<table>
<tr><td>Patient Name:
  JOHN QUEOR</td><td></td><td>Procedure: BYPASS</td></tr>
<tr><td>Page: 206</td><td></td><td>**DEBRIS**</td></tr>
</table>

Debris
Spread upon the green
Where is the world
What does it mean to me
Where does the value stand
Between brown and gold
Fallen stars and broken glass
Fastened quite loosely
Resting on the chest
Over a very secure safe
Filled way up to the gills
With frayed pictures
With subliminal inscriptions
Of love received
But then lost
On rusted lips

He's got things on his mind
Ashing his cigarette
He's got sadness on his lips
Blowing rings skyward

I just admire him from afar
I put his rings in my pocket

He's got the breeze on his face
Tossing his hair haphazardly
He's got the sun in his eyes
Two dark crystals glistening

I want to suck out his poison
I keep his rings in my pocket

He's got no clue I exist
Ashing his cigarette
He leaves with the breeze
I leave with full pockets

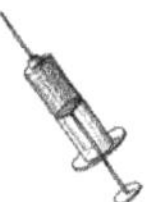

<table>
<tr><td>Patient Name:
  JOHN QUEOR</td><td></td><td>Procedure: BYPASS</td></tr>
<tr><td>Page: 208</td><td></td><td>**WEIGHT OF DESIRE**</td></tr>
</table>

Where do you reside now
Do you often think of me
Am I closed off from your world
By a caution tape boundary
Reminiscent on all of the
Birdsong crime scenes
Of sunlight climbing
With tears glistening
During the fumigation
Of cigarette smoke swirling
During mutual understanding
We were two different pages
Of the same exact book
How far have you come
Are you still the protagonist
Are your dreams blossoming
Are you still drowning
Beneath the weight of desire
To possess that forbidden flower

Soon a patch of tulips will bloom
In the same spot in my parents backyard
Perfectly visible from the kitchen window
Where the breeze will pluck the blossoms
From the thin branches of the twin trees
And the flowers will fall to the ground
To be danced on by the bees
Before being skewed away by the wind
And the whole neighborhood
Will smell of freshly cut grass
The same grass I rolled upon
While getting lost in the sky
Now I wish to have my own
Backyard to sprinkle with tulip seeds
To be visible from the kitchen window
Where the ghosts can look through
To see us rolling in the long grass
Exhaling a different kind of grass
Giggling and watching the clouds
Wondering what to make for dinner
Laughing like dumb teenagers
Kissing like dumb teenagers
Dreaming like dumb teenagers

My dad is so proud of me
My mom says
He has been telling all his friends
About my poetry
I was talking with him today
He told me the hardest part was over
He said that my fears are behind me
And that the world is mine now
But I don't want the world
I always felt like I didn't belong to it
I am grateful for this experience
But this body is just a bag
Holding the dust from my star
That will leap back into the sky
When my skin begins to decay
But I'm so happy he's proud of me
I'm so happy that they both are

To my dearest Ju bobe:

I'm sitting here thinking about our thirty six years of marriage, and all of the happiness you've brought to my life. I thought you were so beautiful when I first saw you at Bison's graduation party and you are still so beautiful now. I knew you were the one, and you always will be for me. You've been such a great mother to our children, and it's been such a pleasure watching them grow with you.

I'm grateful for all the support you provide for not only me, but so many people around us. I look forward to many more years of listening to our favorite music. In

the backyard, just
enjoying each others
company, you're a blessing
in my life, and I love
you very much

Love,
your husband

<table>
<tr><td>Patient Name:
  JOHN QUEOR</td><td></td><td>Procedure: BYPASS</td></tr>
<tr><td>Page: 214</td><td></td><td>**KINTSUGI**</td></tr>
</table>

Elizabeth was melting gold
With a flame she captured
When she escaped Calabasas
And I found myself fortunate
That when my heart was cracking
She shared the liquid with me

I have been slowly hardening
Pushed deeply inside of myself
Suffocating under immense pressure
That I know you can't see

The coal is beginning to shine
And when she pours the gold
Upon me like cool water in the summer
I feel this sense of completeness
Like someone really gets it
Like someone really gets me

I feel like a vintage engagement ring
My woes go back probably further
Than I allow myself to remember
But there's gold where I was broken
And a diamond set in the metal

11·20·23
Oh,
    Come the spring
    Open the door
    to our house of cards
    and let me shuffle in

I know
a royal court awaits
to watch my cups
fill until they spill
over the sides
like two sinking
beneath the bubbles
of a bath
filled up to the brim
I'll kiss your scars
while we collect our coins
and heal the wounds
of the past

KING of PENTACLES.
ACE of CUPS.
KNIGHT of CUPS.
QUEEN of SWORDS
THE LOVERS

<table>
<tr><td>Patient Name:
  JOHN QUEOR</td><td></td><td>Procedure: BYPASS</td></tr>
<tr><td>Page: 217</td><td></td><td>**WARFARIN**</td></tr>
</table>

It has never
Been
Enough

Because
I never
Wanted it
To be

I wasn't ready
I was wasted
Wasting
Away

Dreaming
To fade
But now
I'm awake

Someday
I'll have
Everything

Dear John, (no pun intended)
Where do I even start? It seems
like only yesterday that I met you
at your cousin's graduation party, June
29th, 1985. For me it was love at first
sight. For you, I think, you were
just a handsome man cruising the
party for girls (haha). I had just
turned twenty years old a month
before so I had no idea that my
life would change forever. What an
amazing thirty eight years it has
been. I feel blessed every day. We
have three beautiful, smart and
kind sons. Who could ask for more?
The years have flown by and now
we're empty nesters. Hard to believe,
isn't it? Thank you so much for our
beautiful family and our wonderful
life

    I love you to the moon and back,
        Ju-Babe

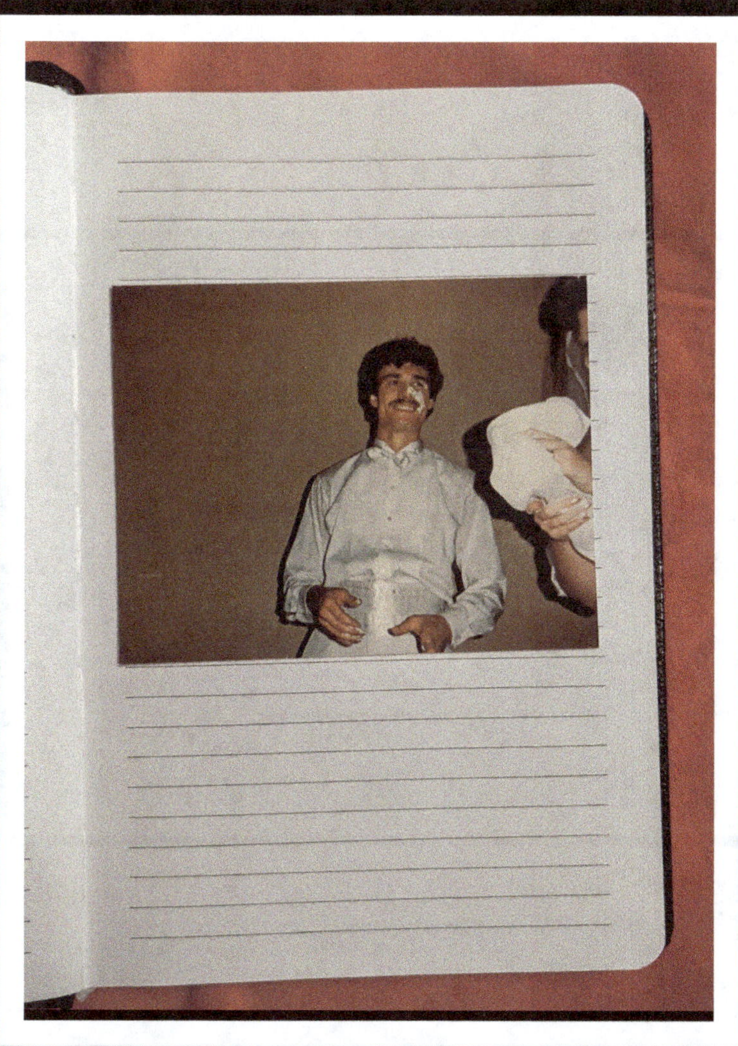

Love is more than I give it credit for
The pain is completely worth it when
My brothers take time to be with me
When my sisters gently reassure me
And my parents say that they're proud
With an embrace lasting
Enough time to melt
The ice caps from my tired shoulders
Where for moments I forget that
Everything is continuously crumbling
I along with everything I've ever known
Will dissolve into the unknown in time
But in this moment everything is fine
I'm surrounded by an incredible warmth
I hope you are spoiled in life too
I hope there's a warmness surrounding you
Love is more than I give it credit for
Even while I fall asleep alone

<table>
<tr><td>Patient Name:
JOHN QUEOR</td><td></td><td>Procedure: BYPASS</td></tr>
<tr><td>Page: 223</td><td></td><td></td></tr>
</table>

ACKNOWLEDGMENTS

Thank you to everyone who sent me pictures! When I thought of the concept for this book, I knew it needed something to offset the tone of bitterness that would shine through. Most of the poetry in this book was written years ago. I thought it would be beautiful to see people who were happy in love and here they are, sealed now in this unique time capsule.

Thank you to my family for supporting me, and getting up from our dinner that day because the lighting was finally right for our picture. Thank you Mom and Dad for giving us an example that love can be successful.

Grandma, thank you for being my number one fan. Thank you for being my PR agent, my traveling salesman, and an inspiration to me.

Thank you to Flor and Indie Earth for all the support and assistance in turning my crazy idea into something crazy beautiful. I can't wait to see what the future has in store for us!

Thank you to everyone who reads this book, I hope you were able to enjoy it!

Thank you to all of the people who I have loved and who have loved me. Without you, this book would not exist.

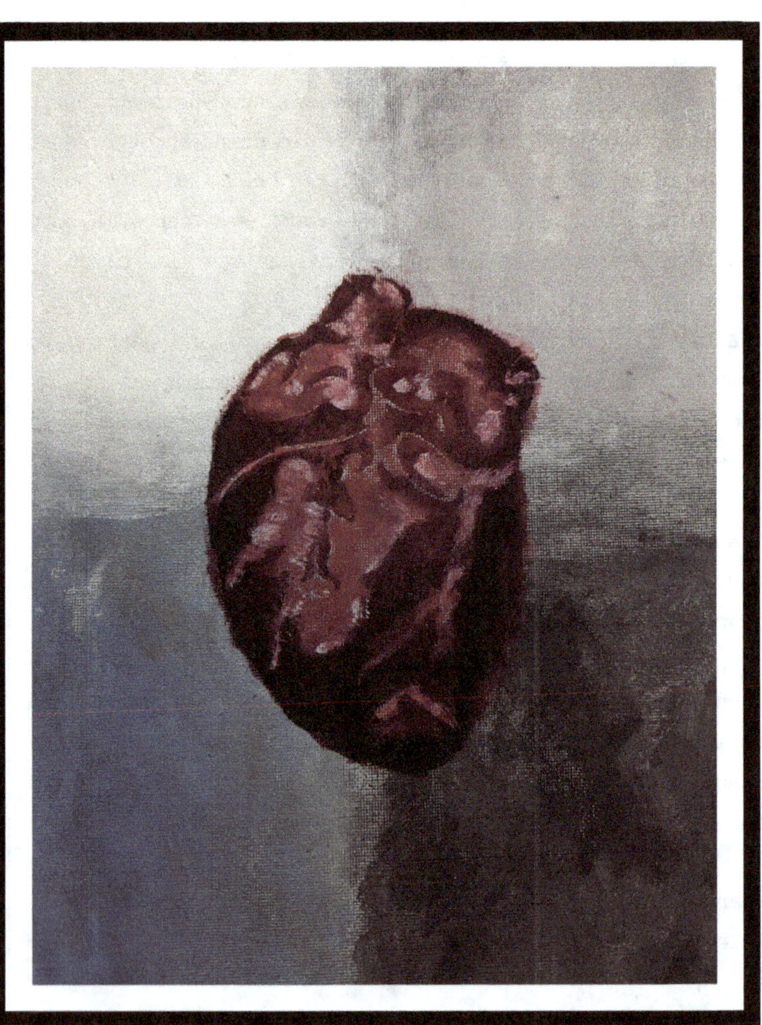

<table>
<tr><td>Patient Name:
JOHN QUEOR</td><td></td><td>Procedure: BYPASS</td></tr>
<tr><td>Page: 225</td><td></td><td></td></tr>
</table>

NOTES & CONTRIBUTIONS

The Coronary Artery Bypass Surgery definition in the Consultation is from Mayo Clinic.

Thank you Angela Pillans for the beautiful artwork on pages 35, 40, 66, 123, and 191! Everything you sent fit the aesthetic so well. I'm excited to have your work in this time capsule!
(You can check out more of Angela's work on www.angelapillans.com)

Thank you Krysta Frost for your photographs on pages 202, 220, and 226. It was so fun spending the day with you capturing the family photos! You've got a great eye and a great heart!

Thank you Matty for the picture of Poe and I and our awesome trip to Boston on page 160. Excited for our next adventure!

Thank you Tara Bonn for our beautiful selfie on the beach and the beautiful time we spend together in every season. Thank you for your photos on pages 81, 99, and 163.

Thank you Tori Gustke for the artwork on page 57, I value your perspective and am happy to know you for all these years.

Thank you Mom and Dad for contributing the beautiful letters. I love you very much!

Once again, thank you to everyone who gave me pictures! They're even more beautiful than I could have imagined!

© Ryan Needle
Instagram: @needlemedia

Here's to young love
turning into smile lines,
and eventually a seaside dream

<table>
<tr><td>Patient Name:
JOHN QUEOR</td><td></td><td>Procedure: BYPASS</td></tr>
<tr><td>Page: 227</td><td></td><td></td></tr>
</table>

MORE FROM JOHN QUEOR

John Queor has also written:

Burnt Lavender (2022)

Resembling A Moth (2023)

John Queor's work has been featured in:

Dreams In Hiding: An Amalgamation of verses and prose

The Spell Jar: Poetry for the Modern Witch

Glow: Self-Care Poetry For The Soul

The Spell Jar II: Book of Shadows

A Winter's Warmth: Short Stories To Keep Out The Cold

<table>
<tr><td>Patient Name:
JOHN QUEOR</td><td></td><td>Procedure: BYPASS</td></tr>
<tr><td>Page: 229</td><td></td><td></td></tr>
</table>

ABOUT THE AUTHOR

John Queor is an equinox, existing equally in the dark and light. He lives in a tower in Central New York, and spends quite a bit of his time writing poetry in the light of the moon. John's poetry fixates on the dualities of everyday life, the sheer appreciation for the petals as well as the thorns.

Connect with John on Instagram:

@johnnyqu33r

@johnnyisjournaling

<table>
<tr><td>Patient Name:
JOHN QUEOR</td><td></td><td>Procedure: BYPASS</td></tr>
<tr><td>Page: 231</td><td></td><td></td></tr>
</table>

ABOUT THE PUBLISHER

Indie Earth Publishing is an author-first, independent co-publishing company based in Miami, FL. A publisher for writers by a writer, Indie Earth offers the support and technical assistance of traditional publishing without asking writers to compromise on their creative freedom. Each Indie Earth Author is a part of an inspired and creative community. For more titles from Indie Earth, or to inquire about publication, please visit:

www.indieearthbooks.com

Instagram: @indieearthbooks

For direct inquires, please email:
indieearthpublishinghouse@gmail.com